Lucy Beatrice Malleson was born in Upper Norwood on February 15, 1899. During the First World War, Malleson's father lost his job, and although her mother wanted her to train as a teacher, Malleson learned secretarial skills so that she could earn an immediate income for the family. From the age of seventeen onwards, she wrote verse and short pieces for *Punch* and various literary weekly publications. During her early years as a secretary, she began to produce novels. Her first crime novel was published in 1927 under the pseudonym Anthony Gilbert, and she went on to write over seventy novels as well as a number of radio plays for the BBC. She valued her privacy and for many years successfully concealed her identity as the writer of the Gilbert novels. Malleson's novels evince a liberal – often feminist – social consciousness and great empathy for the down-and-out and socially marginalised. She lived in or around London for most of her life, and died in 1973.

By the same author
writing as Anthony Gilbert

The Woman in Red
Murder by Experts
Death at Four Corners
Murder is a Waiting Game
and many more

Three-a-Penny

Three-a-Penny

Lucy Malleson

WEIDENFELD & NICOLSON

First published in Great Britain in 1940 by Faber & Faber Ltd

This edition published in 2019 by Weidenfeld & Nicolson
A division of the Orion Publishing Group Ltd
Carmelite House
50 Victoria Embankment
London, EC4Y 0DZ

An Hachette UK Company

1 3 5 7 9 10 8 6 4 2

© Lucy Malleson 1940
Introduction © Sophie Hannah 2019

This memoir was originally published under the pseudonym
Anne Meredith.

The right of Lucy Malleson to be identified as the author
of this work has been asserted in accordance with the
Copyright, Designs and Patents Act 1988.

A CIP catalogue record for this book
is available from the British Library.

ISBN (Mass market paperback) 978 1 4746 1328 6
ISBN (eBook) 978 1 4746 1329 3

Typeset at The Spartan Press Ltd,
Lymington, Hants

Printed and bound in Great Britain by Clays Ltd,
Elcograf S.p.A.

www.orionbooks.co.uk
www.weidenfeldandnicolson.co.uk

DOROTHY SAYERS (to the Author): You must remember, Anthony Gilbert, that although authors are three-a-penny to us, they are quite exciting to other people.

To my friend
JOHN RHODE
who
(whether he realises it or not) suggested
that this book should be written

Introduction by Sophie Hannah

Do most readers read a book's introduction at the beginning, or at the end and only once they've read the book itself? And is that a question that should concern the writers of introductions? Probably not. It's funny, though – I've written many forewords, and I've never before felt the urge to say what I'm going to say now: please consider reading this introduction at the end, and only once you've read Lucy Malleson's wonderful and intriguing memoir.

Why? Well, I think this is rather a mysterious book, though I don't for a moment believe that its author intended it to be. It's riveting but also puzzling, and, to my mind, the mystery has two layers. The first layer – the uppermost mystery, as it were – is this: is there anything peculiar here at all, or am I imagining it? (You will certainly have a view on this once you've read *Three-a-Penny*, so if you would like to be my sidekick and help me solve this mystery, and the next one that I haven't told you about yet, then you should definitely read the book first.)

For clarity, then, the first mystery is this: is this book

a perfectly straightforward account of Malleson's life, with nothing remarkable about it apart from the more interesting biographical details, or is there something in it to be puzzled over and wondered about?

As all avid whodunnit and thriller fans know, cliff-hangers are essential to the genre, as is an effort to ensure that every aspect of the narrative is absolutely clear unless it is intended to be alluringly suspenseful and part of the mystery. So let me leave you hanging on to the edge of that cliff for a while in order to tell you some known facts about Lucy Malleson.

She was born in Upper Norwood in 1899, the daughter of a stockbroker and cousin of the actor and screen-writer Miles Malleson. She was a pupil at the St Paul's School for Girls in Hammersmith and remained in London her whole life. Her family found itself in dire financial straits during the First World War when Malleson's father lost his job, and from that point on, Malleson was acutely aware of the dangers of impending poverty and felt duty-bound to earn as much money as she could to support her family. Much of this memoir is focused on her resolve and determination to succeed in creating a lucrative professional life as a secretary and office worker, working for such organisations as the Red Cross, the Ministry of Food, and the Coal Association.

At the same time, the true love of her life was writing. As a teenager, she wrote regularly for *Punch* magazine and others, and while working as a secretary she started to write novels and plays and to submit them to the appropriate places in the hope of getting them published and produced. It's clear from almost every page of this memoir that she always had a rich inner life, an entirely independent mind and a healthy distrust of adults and all forms of authority.

As a writer, Malleson suffered many failures and rejections, and one of the most refreshing things about *Three-a-Penny* is her tangible determination, which remains as strong as ever even in the face of disappointing results. Malleson is no deluded sugar-coater; she's down to earth, always aware of the harsh realities of life, and often unduly pessimistic (she matter-of-factly says at one point that no one will want to marry her because she's physically unattractive), and yet she wrote this, one of my favourite passages in any book ever, and one of the best and most inspiring definitions of optimism that I've ever read:

So I am still in the ranks of unsuccessful dramatists. Still, I protest that a play that has attracted the attention of one of our leading actor-managers is emphatically not in the same category as a play that has merely gone the rounds and returned with enough rejection slips to paper a cupboard. And I shall go on thinking so until one day Mr. Gielgud or somebody else really puts on a play of mine, after which I can afford to disregard this very minor achievement. The new play, in fact, has just been done and is setting forth on its rounds, and this play may be the turning-point of my career. That's one of the cheerful things about work like ours. If, like me, you still are incorrigibly optimistic, if you know in your heart of hearts that Providence intended you for a success and your main desire in life is to assist Providence to this end, why then you will never see a book with your name on the spine without the eager thought, 'This may be it. This probably is.' And when the book sells no more copies than its predecessor, well, by that time you're always neck-deep in another one, and this one, without doubt, will bring you that elusive fame and financial security that glimmer like distant stars on the far, far horizon.

Malleson's first proper taste of success came when she was offered a contract for her first crime novel *The Tragedy at Freyne*, which she submitted under a male pseudonym: Anthony Gilbert. It was published in 1927, and was only the beginning. As Anthony Gilbert, Malleson published ten novels starring crime-solving politician Scott Egerton, and then in 1936 'Gilbert' published her first crime novel starring her most famous character, Arthur Crook, an unconventional cockney sleuth with a penchant for unethical behaviour in the service of good. She valued her personal privacy and took her Anthony Gilbert identity seriously, at one point even posing for an author photo disguised as a man.

Murder by Experts, Crook's debut, was a big success, and Scott Egerton was immediately dropped as a character;

Malleson concentrated on Crook from then on, writing a further fifty novels in which he featured. In addition to the Gilbert novels, she wrote twenty-one novels under the name Anne Meredith that were not mystery novels, though some of them were 'inverted crime novels', revealing who had committed what crime and why right at the start.

This memoir was originally published under the Meredith name. Malleson also published many stories in *Ellery Queen* magazine and had twenty-five radio plays broadcast. One of her novels inspired the 1945 movie *My Name is Julia Ross*. She was an early member of the The Detection Club, alongside Agatha Christie and Dorothy L. Sayers, and she was the club's General Secretary for a period. Interestingly, although one of the recurring themes of *Three-a-Penny* is the difficulties faced by women in that time who wanted to be taken seriously as professionals and treated as men's equals, Anthony Gilbert is not a household name in the way that the Golden Age Queens of Crime are: Christie, Sayers, Margery Allingham and Ngaio Marsh. Experts on the detective fiction of the twenties and thirties tend to view Anthony Gilbert as rather underrated.

Malleson herself seems to underrate her own literary achievement. At the end of this book, she says:

I don't feel guilty that my books don't sell ten thousand copies, though I should love them to, and so would my publishers. When I was young I confidently thought they would; when they didn't I was astounded, but it never occurred to me, when my average sales were 1,250 copies, to abandon writing and do something more lucrative. Besides, one day they may.

Here, though, is the mystery that, for me, is one of the most interesting features of this memoir: given that her creative work and the life of her imagination were the most important and most rewarding parts of Malleson's life, why does she write so little about them in *Three-a-Penny*? There's a fascinating passage in which she talks about a transformative experience that inspires her to change her plan to write a disposable thriller with no literary merit and instead try to write the very best thriller she could, but apart from that she gives the reader very little insight into the creative imaginations of Anthony Gilbert and Anne Meredith.

Why not? Wasn't that creative process what her life was mainly about? Is her reticence on this front an attempt to keep private the thing that mattered most to her, or did she assume that readers would not care about her plots and characters, how they came into being and what they meant to her, given that she was an author with only modest sales?

This mystery, unsolvable, only serves to make me want to read all the Malleson novels I haven't yet read, and reread the ones I have read. I hope it has the same effect upon all who read it.

Chapter One

The uncle, who was also my godfather, and whose christening present had been a seed-pearl locket on a gold chain, had also at some time or another given me a pair of Indian silver bangles. Sitting on the floor of my mother's room, I played with these, jangling them like handcuffs, rolling them like hoops. My parents watched me speculatively.

'She has my father's forehead,' observed my mother.

'She has my family's mouth,' my father countered.

'She has a distinct look of the Woods about her when she laughs,' insisted my mother.

'She's remarkably like my sister, M——, at times,' said my father firmly.

I put aside my playthings. It had dawned upon me that they were talking about me.

'I am like myself,' I announced truculently, 'and everything I have is all my own.' Then I went back to my bracelets.

★

I was at that time about four years old.

God lived in the sky, whence he saw everything. Even if you could conceal your doings from the grown-ups, you could not escape the abiding vigilance of God. Not only could He see but He could hear, even the things you only said in a whisper, such as 'Nurse is a beast' or 'I don't care' when they told you you had been rude and had hurt Mother's feelings. God kept an enormous book, like the one at Cradock, the butcher's, in which thousands and thousands of entries were made. Cradock made out his bills once a month and Father opened them and said: We shall be ruined. Just look at this. God presented His bill when you died, and if you had done wrong you went to hell for ever. Hell was like a glorified nursery grate on which people lay, always, in imagination's eye, decorously dressed in outdoor clothes, perpetually burning yet never consumed.

Yet God could be kind. He could listen even to little children, as the grown-ups told you He could. In spite of their perplexing ways, the grown-ups were sometimes right. There was the affair of the nursery tablecloth. Myself and Christopher, aged four and five-and-a-half, had dinner in the nursery sitting one either side of the table. I found, with a quite unaccountable sense of shock, that the tablecloth had a raw edge, a thing I had never seen on a cloth before.

'Christopher, there isn't a hem on my cloth.'
'Isn't there? Let's see. No more there is.'

8

'I don't like it,' I said disapprovingly.

'We can't do anything, can we?'

'We might ask God about it.'

One absorbed God, as one absorbed milk from one's bottles. There had never been a time when one was so small one hadn't known about Him, without ever remembering how one knew. Anyway, there it was. One could ask God about it. God could only be addressed with folded hands and shut eyes. For ordinary prayers, of course, one knelt down, but this was dinner, and it was forbidden to leave one's chair until the meal was over. So – eyes shut, hands folded – 'Please, God...'

Then Nurse, who had gone downstairs for a minute, came bustling back.

'All that fat gone?' said Nurse. 'Well, you don't want to have to eat it for tea, do you?'

It was a fine afternoon and the daisies had come out all over the lawn. One of the incredible things about the grown-ups was the way they always wanted to cut the daisies down. And besides the daisies there were some plums in the long grass of the orchard, smooth eau-de-nil plums each with a bright drop of gum on its head, that gave them the appearance of goblins. There was a pear tree, also, with a low branch where two could sit abreast and drive and drive into the world to come. Tablecloths, hemmed or unhemmed, were of small importance. Still, tea-time came; the sun lay in sheets of gold over the

lawn, the syringa was out and so were the roses. But the
cups of milk and the slices of bread-and-butter waited.
Up in the nursery one remembered the cloth, lifted the
hem, stared and stared. So it was true about God – He
did hear. While you played in the garden, somehow – not
for four-year-olds to question how – He had had that
cloth hemmed. You could pass your fingers all round the
border, you wouldn't find a raw edge anywhere. And it
was the same cloth, too, because the stain where you had,
in spite of care, made a splotch of gravy, was under your
cup of milk. It would never be difficult now to believe
in the miracles – the Feeding of the Five Thousand or
the Turning of Water into Wine. God was true. You knew
it, not because the grown-ups said so, but because you'd
proved it for yourself.

Mother was one of eight sisters, of whom seven were
still living. The one who had died had been a little saint
from the first, too good for this world; her picture was
in Grandfather's house, a grave little girl, with fair hair
drawn off her face and secured in a blue velvet snood.
The others were, miraculously, each one quite different.
Mother's special one was Aunt Charlotte. Aunt Charlotte
had been the dashing member of the troupe; she had put
on a swinging cloak and a cavalier hat with a curling
feather and had walked down Bond Street, unaccom-
panied, where she had been waylaid by an artist, who
wanted to paint her.

'Your Aunt Charlotte asked for these adventures,' said

Mother. But you could see Aunt Charlotte was really rather proud of the incident.

Then there was Aunt Beryl, who was married and had a little girl called Maud, whom you disliked heartily, because at five years old she did wonderful needlework; her cottons never tangled or became grey with dirt, and the finished needlecase or handkerchief sachet was always good enough to be sent out as a birthday or Christmas present to one of the aunts. Also, when she came to stay, she always piped up, Mummy shall I put on my pinny? the instant she came in from a walk. No self-respecting child could like those pinafores, stiff white piqué garments, with frilled sleeves, tieing round the neck with a tape that always got starched in the wash and rubbed your skin raw. There was another cousin, an older one, who had been born in China, but who was disappointingly like everyone else in spite of that glamorous fact. She was fair and wore blue sailor suits with anchors embroidered on the pockets, and white serge vests edged with blue, just as you did yourself; and she had exquisite manners and played cribbage with her grandmother when she was nine years old. There was a picture of her doing it in the family photograph album.

Christopher was a good subject for the camera, but I usually contrived to look cross, wearing a starched white hat on the top of my round head, mouth set like a vice.

There was another married aunt called Victoria, who was delicate and very elegant, and known to the family as The Princess, and there were two more unmarried ones,

Kate, who was religious and my godmother, and Isobel, who was very, very pretty and inclined to be strict. The unmarried ones used to come and stay. On those mornings you were allowed to go down to the dining-room at breakfast, and Aunt Charlotte − it was generally Aunt Charlotte − would cut off the top of her egg and let you eat it out of her silver spoon. There was no nonsense about children having a whole egg apiece for breakfast in those days. The eggs were boiled in a silver egg-boiler, lighted by methylated spirits; the top of this boiler was decorated by a swan, which was queer, if you stopped to think about it, since they were hen's and not swan's eggs. The swan fascinated me. It was, in fact, the trade-mark of my beginnings as a writer.

Mother was going to take me out, but she was not quite ready. It might be twenty minutes or half an hour to wait. I must be a good girl and sit quiet and not get in a mess − my capacity for getting into a mess in about thirty seconds was notorious.

'Very well,' I agreed. 'Then I will write a story.'

'What about?'

'A silver swan. That's what it shall be called. The Silver Swan.'

Mother went away; I looked round for paper; I already had a pencil. But the exercise books with mottled covers, ruled in narrow double lines, had been put away; in any case they were intended for pot-hooks and capital letters and the copying of mottoes. A stitch in time saves nine. Look before you leap. Be just before you are generous.

The wall-paper offered no assistance. It had a heavy pattern of nursery rhymes from floor to ceiling, not a clear space anywhere on which to write a rhyme of one's own.

I was a very good girl; I sat where I was and wrote the story in my mind. It was an exciting story about three children, a boy and two girls, who escaped from their parents and set out to have adventures. The children's names were Christopher, Lucy and Joan. Christopher, the eldest, and Joan, the youngest, followed the lead of their intrepid sister, Lucy. She has a fine horse that she rides bareback, but they are only mounted on cows and hang on to their horns. Lucy shakes a careless rein, rushes down canyons, up mountains, leaps abysses, swims foaming torrents. The Indians who, armed with tomahawks, have been after her scalp and those of Christopher and Joan, have instead themselves been scalped by the courageous white girl's cunning, and she is riding back with their scalps hanging at her belt, one of those belts you see in shops with a silver buckle and scalloped edges. The village turns out to greet her; she has feathers in her hair. It is a wonderful story, and it is just finished when Mother comes in.

'Did you write your story, darling?'

'Yes, Mummy.'

'Where is it?'

'I wrote it in my head.'

Mother looks disappointed. 'I thought you were going to write it down.'

'Oh no. I shall remember it quite well without that.'

'But other people might like to read it.'

I am horrified. It's an odd reflection that grown-up authors always want their stories read by as many people as possible, but before you are old enough to be greedy for fame, and before the thought of money has entered your calculations, you get gooseflesh at the bare thought of anybody else reading what you have written. For these stories are intensely private; they are nobody else's affairs. The grown-ups govern practically everything; you aren't supposed to have any secrets from them or even to want to; but they can't turn out your mind as they turn out your play-cupboard.

'What was it about?'

Rather reluctantly I outlined the plot.

'But you can't ride, darling; and it wasn't very kind to give the others cows. If there was only one horse Christopher ought to have it.'

I decided that next time it might be better for the Indian Chief, Silver Swan, to scalp Daddy and Mummy at the beginning of the story; then the three of them can go on having adventures for ever.

Joan had arrived some time ago, one couldn't make out from where.

'Where *did* she come from, Mummy?'

'The doctor brought her.'

'Where did he find her?'

'In his home.'

'I see.' A long pause. 'Do doctors always find babies in their homes?'

'Yes, always. I expect Dr Bunn has found hundreds.'

'Then, Mummy,' a wail of real anguish now, 'how on earth did he know which was the right one for us?'

'Run away, darling. Nice little girls don't ask so many questions.'

'I'm not a nice little girl. You told me so yesterday.'

Presently elucidation came. 'Do the babies have labels on them, Mummy?'

'Yes, darling, I expect so.'

'But you're not sure?'

Poor harassed Mother! And poor me! Followed days of anxious brooding. Suppose, after all, we HADN'T GOT THE RIGHT BABY? I disliked it, anyhow. It was pink and laughing and had golden hair and everybody loved it. Nurse dressed it in its pelisse and its satin bonnet trimmed with swansdown, and said, 'Will you give me one of your curls, lovey?' And Baby, that sickening creature, said: Ah! Goo! And Nanny got a pair of scissors and cut off a curl. Then she turned, saying sharply: 'Well, Miss Lucy, do you mean to say you haven't put on your own hat yet? A big girl like you!'

It was winter and the snow fell; bitterly, bitterly cold, but not too cold for walking, said Mother.

'Wrap them up warm and take them to the Park,' she told Nurse.

Nurse was small and dark and Welsh, with a hard hand. She grabbed me by the wrist and said: 'Now hold on to the pram as I told you, or it'll be the worse for you.'

Outside, the wind was so cold it stung. I wore a white silk mesh veil over my face, that kept getting into my mouth. I had a black astrachan fez with a tarboosh, and a red coat, speckled with white, like the snow. All the way to the Park I cried with the cold, steadily, hopelessly, remorselessly. Ladies in furs said, 'What a shame! Poor little thing!' Nurse pushed the pram as though she were a machine. When we reached the Park she anchored it by some railings and went into a little house marked Ladies. She told me to come in, too. My tears momentarily ceased. I had never been inside one of these little houses. But once there Nurse seated herself squarely on the wooden seat, plucked me across her knee, and went through the familiar ritual of lifting clothes and undoing buttons. Smack! Smack! Smack!

'I'll give you something to cry for, my lady,' said Nurse.

I stopped crying in sheer astonishment. I had never realised they built little houses in public parks just for this. I was so much surprised I made the rest of the journey in awed and crestfallen silence.

The God business presented problems. If there was, as a socialist housemaid (she only stayed her month) declared, one law for rich and another for the poor, certainly there was one commandment for the adult and another for the child. Lying was a dreadful crime in the young;

but grown-ups lied with impunity. They said 'Not at home' when they were sitting in the drawing-room as large as life and twice as brazen; they said a thing happened the other day when it was more than a year ago; they said: If you make any more noise I shall go mad; but when you went on, just to see what madness was like, they merely 'gave you something to yell for' and went on as usual.

Then there was the Workhouse Mystery. One day Daddy received a number of envelopes, and when he had opened them he flung them on the table, saying quite definitely: 'We shall have to go to the Workhouse. There's no question about it. We may as well get ready.'

Get ready! Ominous phrase. Probably it meant starting in about ten minutes. You were always being told to get ready, and the result invariably was that within ten minutes you went out. It wasn't much time, for there was a lot to be done. One had one's own personal packing to attend to. Jumbo, the elephant, for whom Mother had made – oh, how many fresh tails of bits of cloth, which you stuffed with torn-up newspapers – Gerald, the liver-coloured flannel pig on wheels, as big as an Aberdeen terrier, who squeaked instead of grunting when his stomach was prodded; books and chalks and the golliwog with one eye missing; only one doll, and that a minute one called Rossie, with only one leg. Then a frantic hunt for string to tie up one's pet books – *A Peep Behind the Scenes* (Aunt Lucy, I think the pasture is very green indeed); *The Story of the Robins; The Story of a Rat* by A.L.O.E. (A Lady of England) in a bright pink penny edition; two or three cherished fairy tales, also in penny editions; *Aesop's Fables*, with the pictures coloured by hand, in chalk; *The Wide Wide World*, *The Diamond Fairy Book*, *The Story of the Brownies*, the *Louis Wain Cat Book*, the linen book preserved from childhood – Monday's child is fair of face, Tuesday's child is full of grace, Wednesday's child is full of woe … One stopped there. One was a Wednesday's child oneself, an Ash Wednesday's child at that. The picture represented three clowns walking uphill and one of them falling down and breaking his nose. Christopher was a Friday's child – kind and giving. His picture was a little boy in a Lord Fauntleroy suit offering his biscuit to a dog.

Nurse (a different nurse by this time) said: 'What on earth are you doing, Miss Lucy?'

And me, very important and busy and hot: 'We're going to the Workhouse, Nurse, in about ten minutes, and I simply must take Jumbo and Gerald and all the rest.'

Why on earth did Nurse laugh so? She called to Edith, the house parlour-maid, who laughed too.

'Are you coming to the Workhouse, Nurse?'

'Me, Miss Lucy? They wouldn't have me.'

So there was something to be said for Workhouses after all.

And then, when one was ready and eager to start, nothing happened. There were lessons and a walk the same as usual, and when you said in perplexity, 'But

18

what about the Workhouse?' Mother said, under her breath, 'Poor lambs!' and aloud, 'Daddy thinks perhaps we needn't go just yet, after all.'

A year later there was the mysterious affair of the Creepy-Crawlies. At the foot of the garden stood the rubbish-heap, an aggregation of cut grass, twigs, sawn branches, all the flotsam and jetsam of years of enthusiastic gardening. The Creepy-Crawlies lived in the rubbish-heap, lovely black and red ones, with innumerable legs, and long lithe slippery bodies, moving with a rapid, gliding motion, that made them astoundingly difficult to catch. If you weren't very quick, they dived head first into the rubbish and were lost. Digging them out was hopeless; they fell through the heap like stones over a cliff. Mummy had people to tea, a lot of uninteresting old ladies; not nona-genarians, precisely, but ladies quite as old as Mummy herself, some of them, perhaps, older still. Certainly one had white hair. Cook had been in one of her approach-able moods and had lent a deep enamel dish in which the Creepy-Crawlies could be put, when caught. The hunt went on seriously until the dish was half-full, with a worm or two for good weight. Worms had to be a certain size, a rather majestic kind known as King Worms. Every now and then Christopher would say, 'That's not a King,' and out it would go. Baby didn't play on the rubbish-heap. Baby didn't like these messy places where, naturally, you were bound to get dirty. Mother said Baby was going to take after her side of the family. I still had fugitive doubts as to her being in the right house, though Christopher assured her earnestly that he remembered perfectly well the circumstances of her birth.

'I was sitting in the dining-room,' he said, 'and the doctor came in, carrying a black bag. He said: Is Mrs Malleson ready for that baby? and he rushed up the stairs. And a little bit later Nurse came down and said: You've got another little sister. I suppose she didn't know I'd seen it arrive in the bag.'

When the tin was half-full one of us said, 'Suppose, well, what do you think about letting THEM see the Creepy-Crawlies?'

The suggestion was debated and approved. It must be pretty dull sitting in a stuffy drawing-room on a lovely summer afternoon, with a garden outside, full of living things. We stole softly across the lawn. The french windows of the drawing-room opened on to a conservatory, whose door stood open. We came through the forest of red geraniums under glass, Christopher pushed the window wide and held up the pie-dish like an offering to the gods, while I cried dramatically: 'Look!'

The effect was electrical. Everybody looked, including one of the red Creepy-Crawlies, who reared himself up and peered over the edge of the tin. There was instant panic. In those days skirts were worn long and full. Ladies leaped up, gathering their bunchy folds about them; they gesticulated and shrieked. Mother said: Take those away – quickly. Christopher looked pained; I simply couldn't understand what it was all about. The red Creepy-Crawly was so much taken aback that he fell out of the tin on to the carpet and vanished. The tumult increased, led by this time by me, who regardless of the visitors, was down on all fours, crying, 'We'll lose him. We'll lose him,' and crawling rapidly round the carpet, plump hindquarters in frilled white drawers offering a tempting target to the outraged guests.

The Creepy-Crawly knew what he was about. He had simply vanished. I was red with crawling and disappointment. I wanted to make sure he hadn't crept up one of the ladies' dresses. The visitors shrank from the exploring hand as though it were the Creepy-Crawly himself. Somehow Mother got both culprits outside, with the tin of exhibits, and set about calming the drawing-room. Christopher and I moved, amazed and dejected, over the lawn. Things had happened so fast it was necessary to take a moment to adjust one's mind.

At last Christopher spoke. 'They didn't like them,' he said.

'*They* didn't like the ladies,' I mourned. 'We ought to have thought of that. They wouldn't, of course.'

But consolation awaited us when we returned to the rubbish-heap. Sticking out, about a foot from the top, was an odd scaly protrusion, pointed at the end. We watched; it made a slight movement. I picked up a stick and gave it a sharp rap. Instantly it disappeared. A minute later the other end shoved its way through the top. A snake! A real snake! The tin of Creepy-Crawlies was put on the path, its occupants thankfully making their getaway. The pair of us climbed the pile, but the snake had gone.

'If we could find it we might show it to THEM,' I panted. 'They'd be sure to love THAT.'

'They might not,' said sceptical Christopher. 'With Grown-Ups, You Never Can Tell.'

'Well, anyhow Daddy'll like it. He's not a lady.'

Daddy was due in about half an hour. As he came into the house he was beset by two howling savages.

'Daddy, there's a snake in the garden.'

'It's a real snake. It hissed at us.'

'Probably it's poisonous.'

Daddy reacted magnificently. He snatched up a stick and went into the garden, without even waiting for his tea. Christopher and I followed, praying desperately that the snake would behave like a gentleman. And the snake justified our warmest expectations. He was in the path and when he heard us coming he reared up, and hissed.

Daddy said, in a queer voice I didn't know, 'Keep back, you two! Keep back, I say,' and went for the snake, with stick upraised. The snake must have recognised the voice, for he gave one rapid glide, and was under the fence in to the next-door garden.

'That was a viper,' said Daddy, looking a bit white.

'And you've given it to the people next door! Oh, Daddy.'

Daddy said he'd better warn them.

'You can tell them, if they don't want it, they can give it back to us,' I offered, hopefully. But that evening old Mr Parker sent in word that his gardener had killed the snake. Christopher and I were furious. 'It was our snake,' we said. After that, we realised it's never safe to trust Grown-Ups. When we collected slugs we put them where no one would think of looking for them. It was a pity the adults should lose so much fun, but it was their own fault. We loved to watch those slowly swivelling horns, with the eyes at the tip.

'Do you suppose they can see us? Do they know we like them?'

It was a pity slugs couldn't talk. A pity, too, that there were no longer any asses like Balaam's, that spoke to him in the way. Actually, all the best animals were in the Bible – the whale that swallowed Jonah, the fish with the money in its mouth, Bel's dragon, Elijah's bears, and David's lions and tigers. There was practically nothing left for nowadays.

And then the Dancing Bear happened.

Chapter Two

He came out of the blue, walking down the dusty road, with a leather belt round his waist, and attached to the belt a length of steel chain, and holding the other end of the chain a little dark man. Another man, taller, more English, walked on the pavement. The bear came through the gate, round the monkey-puzzler in the central bed, and halted in front of the dining-room windows. There were three of these, reaching almost to the ground. The bear reared himself on his hind-legs; he was a very pale coloured bear, with a patchy hide. At a command from one of the men he began to dance. It was queer dancing, not set steps, just a jigging shifting from one leg to the other.

'He doesn't dance very well,' suggested Christopher.

I rushed to the defence of the miracle. 'That's all you know.'

'How much do you know about dancing?'

'You only know about boy dancing. This is bear dancing. Of course it's different.'

The bear was very old, very tired, almost too senile to realise what was expected of him. Moreover, he had trudged several miles under a broiling sun. Jig-jig, jig-jig, he lurched from side to side, his big fore-paws waving aimlessly, his beautiful bear's head nodding as he moved. He kept it up for a little while, then gratefully sank back to all fours. Daddy gave the men something, and I pleaded, 'Couldn't he come in and have tea?'

What an experience and what a thing to boast about!

'We had a bear to tea on Wednesday!'

But everybody laughed, and the old bear turned and shambled through the gate, the tall man following him, smoking a cigarette, and with his hands in his pockets, as though bears were as common as aunts.

'Let's play bears. I'll be the bear and you can be the man.'

'No, I'll be the bear.'

Eventually we took it in turns. The bears showed all manner of enterprise.

Presently I protested. 'You're doing boy dancing again.'

'Pooh! So would the bear, if he knew how.'

The tumult grew. Nurse said: 'Stop it, for goodness' sake. My head's something chronic.'

So presently we played at being dogs, crawling about under the table and sniffing at one another, until Nurse stopped that, too.

I couldn't get over the bear; it was a better miracle than the tablecloth, the best miracle there had ever been. While Nurse hustled me into bed, I talked incessantly.

Was it a father bear? Or a mother bear? Were there any baby bears? How much would Daddy have had to pay for the bear to come to tea? Did it sleep in a bed with one of the men or have a bed all to itself? Would it be possible to follow it up tomorrow and see it dance again?

Nurse said: 'Give over, do, and let me brush your teeth.' Then she said: 'Now then, prayers, and look smart.' Mother generally heard one's prayers, but presumably that night Mother was out.

I knelt down. God bless Daddy and Mummy and Christopher and Joan and Nurse and all friends kind and dear and thank You for the bear, and please, please bless the bear, and I'm sorry for being naughty (that was part of the nightly ritual whether one's conscience were troubled or no) and please take care of the bear, and make me a good girl, and let there be another bear soon, for Jesus Christ's sake, Amen.

Then I got into bed and Nurse put out the light and I lay and thought about the bear. I sang a sort of paean to it. Oh ravishing, oh exquisite, oh perfect bear. Oh, thrice-blessed men who travelled with it. Why hadn't Daddy thought of having a bear instead of going every day to the city? But perhaps bears cost too much. That was probably the reason. Some time later Nurse came in to see if I was asleep. Emily, the house parlour-maid, was with her. You shut your eyes and hoped Nurse would be deceived, because it was naughty to be awake when she came in, unless you had a pain.

Nurse was telling Emily about my praying for the bear. 'Little comic,' said Nurse. Emily replied, 'I believe they train them something cruel. Hot plates and nails ... Of course they're not English ...'

I heard her and chuckled to myself. They must think me a big silly to believe that sort of story. Grown-Ups were unkind to one another – I had once found Mother crying over a letter – and they could ill-treat children. Only last week Nurse and Emily had told one another juicily about a little boy whose father had beaten him to death in a drunken mood (they had forgotten I was playing behind the chair); but all that was different. No one would be cruel to an *animal*. It simply wasn't possible.

I knew better a year later, when the new cook caught a mouse and put it on the kitchen fire. I was nearly hysterical with rage and misery.

'It was dead, darling,' Mother promised me.

'Perhaps it wasn't really dead,' I wept. 'Perhaps it was only pretending to be dead.' Like oneself pretending to be asleep when Nurse came in.

'No, it was really and truly dead.'

But I wasn't to be so easily comforted. I had caught Grown-Ups out before. You couldn't believe them; they had a different kind of truth from yours. And then I heard of a boy who had stoned a starving cat, and realised that God had been right, after all, in creating hell, because nothing else would be bad enough.

★

28

Hell! One thought more about it as one got older, until the time came when it seemed inevitable. There was a hymn you had in church sometimes:

> *My God, I love Thee, not because*
> *I hope for Heaven thereby,*
> *Nor yet because who love Thee not*
> *Are doomed eternally.*

Loving God! The idea was absurd. One's only hope was to think about the future as little as possible, and remember the 'objectionable' answer of Charlotte Brontë's heroine, 'I must keep in good health and not die.'

This preoccupation with hell was the more strange because it wasn't one's parents who talked about it. Perhaps, years ago, there had been a nurse – and certainly in one of the old illustrated Bibles there had been horrific pictures of demons with tails and horns and smoking tridents tormenting naked and doomed men. It was impossible to remember when this deathly fear began, but for a long time now, when you lay awake in the dark, you wondered desperately whether you could ever get accustomed to the torment and the flame. They said you could get used to anything in time, but if you couldn't even get accustomed to toothache, but had to have Daddy to come and take you in his arms and tell you how he once put raw whisky on a cut and how frightfully it hurt, so that he washed it off again, until gradually you forgot about the toothache and went to sleep, it wasn't in the least likely you would ever get used to hell.

Later, much later, an Anglican priest, dilating on the subject, said: Imagine a great ball of iron as large as the world, and suppose that once every thousand (or million) years a dove comes flying past and sweeps away a flake no larger than a feather, think of the billions of years it would take before that ball was dissolved, and at the end of that time eternity would be no shorter.

That was years afterwards, but still one was haunted by terror.

Sundays were very serious days. On Saturday nights all the toys and story-books were put away till Monday. Even if you were too small to attend church you must not take your doll for a walk or play with the doll's house the old Miss Cranes had given you, that had four rooms and a real staircase and tiny miniature pictures in gilt frames on the walls, and dolls, that Mother had dressed for a father and a mother. You could not even play with the rigid china doll in her tin bath that you had bought yourself for a penny at the Penny Bazaar. Your Sunday amusements were *Darton's Sunday Pleasure Book* and Cook's *Texts*.

Cook was a robust little Scotswoman, a sturdy Plymouth Sister, and she had little pink books containing a text for every day of the year. Contexts from the Old Testament were indicated by the name of the book, but no help at all was given if the text came from the New.

If you found five texts in one day you had done pretty well. Darton's was altogether more difficult, but more intriguing. Sections would be headed Birds of the Bible or Crops of the Bible, and a series of questions appended.

How often are sparrows mentioned in the Bible and where?

Through what field did the disciples pass on the Sabbath Day?

Also it had pictures that might be coloured by hand. But once when I decided to give a harvester black and white spotted pantaloons, after the manner of the clown on the pier the previous summer, Mother was shocked. She said it wasn't at all suitable. So one submissively returned to the letterpress.

Sitting in the conservatory waiting for Sunday dinner – roast beef, Yorkshire pudding and vegetables, with chocolate blancmange to follow – I watched Father attending to his hollyhocks. He had been to church twice already and would go again tonight. On one of the leaves he found a fat caterpillar.

'If this were not a Sunday,' thus he addressed the creature that lay, curled up in instinctive self-defence in the palm of his hand, 'I should slay you. But as it is, I shall put you on my neighbour's hollyhocks.' And over the wall the caterpillar went.

Something, clearly, rejoiced because it was Sunday. But, on the whole, it was a tedious day, the service incomprehensible, the sermon far too long. And excessive fidgeting or talking aloud during the service was penalised by instant removal to bed on one's return, and a second tepid slice of Yorkshire pudding in place of the delicious, creamy, melting chocolate blancmange.

Once there was a diversion. While he was setting light to the incense a piece of hot coal leaped up and burned the vicar's hand, and he was so much disconcerted that he whirled the thurible round his head and it crashed against the vestry wall. But nothing like that ever happened again.

Joan's godmother had sent three guinea-pigs – Marmaduke, Dulcie, and Joy (whose name was subsequently changed to Adolphus, when it became obvious that this was more suitable). Dulcie was small and short-haired; Dulcie was given to me. On the first Sunday afternoon Daddy made a wire-netting pen on the lawn to give the guinea-pigs exercise. He gave them a lot more than he had intended; for the guinea-pigs were lively animals, and all through the long Sunday afternoon Scripture lesson, conducted by Father in the study for the benefit of Christopher and me, Joan, still happily too young to attend, persistently put a shy face round the door.

'Daddy, one of the guinea-pigs has got out.'

Exquisite guinea-pigs, so to relieve the tedium of Sunday afternoon. But by next week the run was so strong and so high they couldn't escape. A cat got two of them in the end. Dulcie was the first victim. She was found in her run, suffocated, but without a mark upon her.

'It was that black cat,' said Emily.

'She thought it was one of her kittens,' suggested Cook. 'Wanted to keep it warm, I expect.'

'If I was a cat and I saw a guinea-pig, I wouldn't think it was a kitten,' I sobbed.

'If you were a cat, you might.'

Cats, obviously, are stupid creatures. Somehow one's never been able to get up much enthusiasm for them since. Besides, they're cruel to mice and moles, and even if it is their nature, it shouldn't be permitted. Children are cured of undesirable tendencies, so why not cats? But that's one of the questions even the grown-ups can't answer.

'Lucy,' said Miss B., lying on the sofa, and holding up a magazine, 'read this.'

I leaned over her shoulder.

'Not so close.'

'I can't see if I'm any further away.'

'I thought not. That's all right. You can go.'

Next Saturday Mother said, 'You're going up to London today, with Daddy.'

'What for?'

'Because you can't see the blackboard at school.'

'That's because I sit in the back row.'

'You're going to have glasses. Then you'll be able to see it from anywhere.'

The oculist was a rather terrifying little old man, with a white moustache. He flashed lenses in front of one's

33

eyes, and said 'Say stop when you can read those letters at the end of the room.' He asked, 'Do you read in bed?'

I said, 'No.'

'I found you reading in bed only yesterday,' expostulated Father.

'I've given it up since then,' I retorted.

Afterwards I was taken for my first and last ride in a hansom cab, and later still given eclairs and lemonade at a Lyons' teashop.

The school, carried on by three sisters, Miss B., Miss Julia, and Miss Amy, was a long way off. A quarter of an hour's smart walking brought you to the tram stop, and it was a penny ride from there. But after a time tram-rides were forbidden, because one afternoon I forgot to alight at the proper stop. The car was sailing right past the school-gates, there was no time to be lost; I looked both ways as I had always been told and jumped.

Miss B. said afterwards that probably the stiff straw hat had preserved me from serious injury, for I alighted on my head; one of the junior mistresses said, characteristically, '*What* a nice hard skull!' But one felt undeniably important, lying in a deck-chair on the lawn, saying, 'I think I'm all right, thank you.' But the stupid woman insisted on sending me home with the junior mistress, who explained everything volubly, and no one listened to my disclaimers, and the net result was that in future one was to walk both ways.

★

A mysterious old gentleman lived next door, and one afternoon, as one dragged home from school, he was standing at the gate and said, 'H'm! Like to come and see my garden?'

It was a wonderful garden, even more colourful than Father's, and much, much larger. He picked a rose for you to take home, and when you got in and explained why you were late, Mother said: 'It was all right with Mr C——, of course, but, as a rule, never go anywhere with old gentlemen.'

'Why not?'

'Because something might happen.'

'What?'

'Never mind. But remember what I've told you. If anyone ever asks you to show him the way anywhere, just say you don't know.'

'Even if I do?'

'Nice old gentlemen don't ask little girls. They ask a policeman.'

'There mightn't be a policeman handy.'

Will one ever understand the adult concept of truth? And if it's rude not to do what visitors ask you, like standing up to recite, or playing 'The Flower Song', how is it that it isn't rude when it's a stranger? There's something in the Bible, too, about being kind to the stranger within your gates. Anyway, what could an old gentleman do? Get you into his own house and cut you to pieces with rawhide whips, perhaps, a fate that frequently threatens the heroes of Christopher's penny dreadfuls. I, of course, read all these. Their feminine counterparts are beneath contempt. *Pansy*: the story of a young life, and *A Brave Young Heart*, the story of a boy who became a fishmonger, through sheer hard work and honesty and good manners. (Now, how fortunate it is that I am naturally observant, quoth Dick, or I should most certainly have spelt fishmonger with a 'u'.) Well, even at eight years old I knew better than that, and Dick was sixteen.

In the schoolroom was a book called *Readings from Great Literature* that contained part of Macaulay's 'Horatius'. The story fired the children's imaginations. They marched round and round the garden, chanting:

> *Oh Tiber, Father Tiber,*
> *To whom the Romans pray,*
> *A Roman's life, a Roman's arms,*
> *Take thou in charge today.*
> *So he spake and, speaking, sheathed*
> *His good sword by his side,*
> *And with his harness on his back*
> *Sprang headlong in the tide.*

One day, up in the attics, we found a number of long bleached palms, and we carried these, waggling gloriously, over our shoulders. But when Father saw us, he explained that they had been blessed, and they had to go back, presumably to moulder in the attics. But we persisted with the Lays, and all bought penny copies in bright orange covers, with print that would have almost defeated a microscope.

Suddenly everything was set for change. We were going to leave Upper Norwood and go to London. Someone else would live in the house with the blue baize door, and hunt in the long grass of the orchard for frogs, and collect the windfalls, and hunt among the scarlet-runners for ladybirds. Every tree in the garden must have its separate farewell; every possible cherry be devoured, stones and all, with a splendid disregard for the possibility of appendicitis.

The last morning was spent playing with the croquet set, because there wouldn't be any facilities for croquet in London.

'Not even a garden?'

'Oh yes, there would be a garden, but only a small one.'

On the way up I read the Lays with absorption. A man who got into the carriage presently looked over my shoulder and then turned to stare at Mother with horror-stricken eyes. I was troubled. Was it possible the Lays were improper? And if so, how was it that the children had been allowed to read them? But perhaps Mother didn't know.

We got out at London at Addison Road Station. I looked up and saw Olympia written in gold letters across a great glass front.

'Olympia,' I said. 'That's where the gods lived.'

Mother said it was nice having such intelligent children.

London, at first, was a disappointment. The house, for one thing, was one of a long terrace, not even semi-detached, and not a patch on the house we had left, that had gardens back and front. Long steps led to the front door, and there was a basement. We rushed to look at the garden and found a squalid little gravel patch, with a cherry-tree in one corner, some sooty laurels, a privet bush by the scullery window and a fig-tree that, like its biblical prototype, bore leaves but no fruit.

The lady-next-door had erected a trellis between the two houses, and effectually screened off her lilac bush. Once, when one leaned out of the fig-tree to pull a tiny scrap of lilac, she appeared, like a human needle, saying furiously, 'What do you think you are doing? Don't you know what happens to little thieves?'

And she never would throw back balls that had bounced over the wall. She said they burnt them, but Christopher thought most likely she sold them and kept the money.

Joan cried that first night in London, but Christopher was very grown-up. He said he liked it, though he had a horrid little room here, compared with the one he had left. But there was electric light on the ground and first floors, that we had never seen before.

★

The new school was not so far off as the old one had been, though during those first days it was easy to lose your way home. It was quite different from Miss B.'s, different and somehow rather shocking. For several of the girls, who were all older than me, used language that would have horrified Mother, and one of them drew indecent diagrams on the blackboard when the mistress was out of the room.

'I expect Lucy loves her new school, doesn't she?'

'Of course I do.' Everybody of proper instincts loved school. And anyway, nobody filled your boots with water or put your hat down the lavatory pan, which was what had happened to one of the other pupils, a big sandy-haired girl with a strong, ugly face.

'But – what did your mother say?'

'She went to see Miss S——.'

'Did she buy you a new hat?'

'Of course.'

Obviously E.'s parents were Quite Rich People.

At this school the clique flourished like a green bay-tree. Coming home at night one saw little gatherings of one's school-mates on the doorsteps of empty houses. They bent their heads together, whispered, and laughed.

'What are they talking about?'

'They're telling one another the way babies are born.'

One could afford to disregard that. One knew. They came in a doctor's black bag, each with a label round its neck. A doctor's house resembled the giants' larders of nursery days, crowds of infants in long clothes hanging on hooks awaiting delivery.

You couldn't pretend I was popular. When the great N.R. Society was formed, no one suggested I should join. One's first intimation of its existence was when a number of class-mates turned up wearing large white buttons, with N.R. embroidered on them in scarlet thread.

'What does that stand for?'

'Wouldn't you like to know?'

At 'break' the N.R.s notified their conscious superiority to the rest of their class-mates by keeping all together and sharing their milk and biscuits. And afterwards they linked arms and galloped up and down the corridor, chanting, 'We belong to the N.R. Society. We belong to the N.R. Society.'

'Silly snobs,' said some one. 'We can form a society, too.'

But it had very little vitality. Forty-eight hours later the N.R.s expelled one of their members – it was the girl with the sandy hair – and she was cajoled into a corner and persuaded to break the oath she had taken never to reveal the secrets of her society, and told us that N.R. stood for Not Rude, and was intended to differentiate its members from the girls who stood about on doorsteps, discussing childbirth. Of its rules I remember nothing, except that if a member could not attend one of the secret meetings, a note must be sent to the leader at least half an hour beforehand.

The cliques flourished for a time. We exasperated our parents by saying we couldn't invite Norma or Joyce or Alice to tea because she belonged to the other side.

'But I know Norma's mother quite well,' our mothers would expostulate.

'You don't want us to be traitors,' we would say, grandly.

There was a Prize Essay Competition that term – My Favourite Book – and I wrote about *The Lays* and won the New Girls' Prize. Almost the only distinction I achieved at that school was a record of always getting ten out of ten for essays, and winning one of the annual prizes in this subject. On the sole occasion I was awarded 9½ out of 10, I protested until I was granted the additional half mark.

Next year the subject was Edward VII, who had died in the previous May, and the year after What I Want to Be. I said a poet, although to date nothing of mine had ever appeared in print. Christopher had beaten me there with some verses in a parish magazine. He also wrote excellent limericks.

> *There was a young lady, whose smile*
> *Would frighten a cow at a mile.*
> *One morning, alas,*
> *She looked in the glass,*
> *And now she's stopped smiling awhile.*

But not even the parish magazine would publish that. I wrote a good deal of very indifferent verse, chiefly about animals, though occasionally I turned my attention to flowers, since all the major poets appeared to have done the same. And an aunt posted a great batch of MSS. to *Little Folks* who, however, politely returned them.

It was Saturday morning, and I had gone into a sweet-shop to buy a pennyworth of mocha caramels. These were a delicious sweetmeat, sold at the amazing rate of four ounces a penny, which meant that you could ask for a ha'porth. Sweetshops objected to weighing out ounces, unless the sweets were a penny an ounce. There was an old gentleman by the counter when I entered, buying a whole pound of cream fondants, an order so lordly that I felt rather shy about my pennyworth. However, he stood back politely and I stepped up. I was wearing my 'holiday' as distinguished from my 'school' hat, a large affair in limp green linen that hung like elephants' ears round my face. While I waited the old gentleman suddenly leaned forward and twitched one of the 'ears' aside.

'So it is a child,' he said. 'Did your mother buy you that hat?'

'She did – of course.'

'These silly women,' said the old gentleman, either to the empty air or to the sales lady. 'Are they ashamed of their children's faces that they want to hide them? You're not ashamed of it, are you?'

That last was to me. I was dumb. Actually, I had never

thought about it. There was something 'odd', not quite 'good form' about girls who speculated as to their own appearance. Even the plainest face can be beautiful, I'd been told, if a beautiful soul shines through the eyes. Anyway, Mother said that there were no girls nowadays to compare with her school-fellows, so elegant, so finely turned-out, so self-assured. I pictured them, a fleet of proud dazzling young Dianas, about to loose a flood of beauty and of grace on an expectant world. They never inked their forefingers, got reports, or bit their nails. Probably they swam through the enchanted air in velvets and furs.

However, seeing that the old gentleman was awaiting a reply, I stammered, with one eye on my caramels: 'No, I wasn't ashamed of it.'

He nodded approval. 'Quite right. Never let anyone make you ashamed, whatever happens. Never mind what you look like, remember it's your face, and no one else in the world has one quite like it. It's one of your chief modes of expression. Be proud of it.'

I didn't know what to make of him. His mere old-gentlemanliness made him a peril and a menace. And meeting him in a sweetshop increased the odds. Because Mother had said, 'If ever they offer you sweets, be sure you refuse them.' Sweets come by in that way had a peculiar effect, one didn't quite understand what. Still, he hadn't offered me a sweet yet. I put out my hand, grabbed my little paper bag, yielded up my hot penny, and dived for the door.

The old gentleman was before me. 'Have one of these,' he said, and opened the mouth of his bag.

So he *was* One of Those, whatever Those might be. I shook my head and tore past him into the sunlight. He came to the pavement edge and shouted after me.

'And burn that hat,' he called. 'Never mind what your mother says, burn it.'

But, naturally, I did nothing of the sort. If I destroyed it, where on earth should I get another?

Chapter Three

I went to St Bride's School just before my twelfth birthday. Actually pupils were not supposed to be admitted until after that date, but it was a matter of a few weeks and I had done well in the entrance examination, so they let me through. Mother bought me a whole new outfit for the occasion. I had a green skirt, very heavy and rather long, a green-and-brown striped flannel blouse with a collar that hooked up on minute hooks all round, and was decorated with a little brown silk bow, finished off with tassels. In order to 'lighten' the whole, for I was a dark child, and my hair was not then the colour I have since taken pains to see it shall become, a collarette was tacked on. These collarettes were narrow strips of embroidery with scalloped borders, costing a penny three-farthings each.

Everything we wore had that odd three-farthings tacked on to it. White woven bodices (made of cotton) that buttoned down the front and always shrank in the wash, so that there were bulges between the buttons, and rapidly blued so that they never seemed really clean, were six three-farthings with short sleeves, and twopence more in the winter, when sleeves were long. If the summer bodices had lasted well, one wore them in the winter, too, with the addition of a pair of 'sleeves', a kind of long woollen mitten, with no hands, but the inevitable scalloped edge, that reached from wrist to elbow. They were never long enough to meet the short sleeves, and I was always cold in that part of the arm that was covered by neither sleeve nor mitten. Bloomers were of the cosy coloured cotton-and-wool variety, that began by being 'fleecy', but after being washed once or twice were as hard as boards; they fastened on the 'trapdoor' model, with a variety of buttons.

I wore grey fabric gloves and my mother told me not to take them off till I reached school. Only common children walked through the streets with bare hands, and anyway, 'Gloves at eight three-farthings are no joke.'

Here, again, I was a year younger than most of my class, and quite incredibly innocent. It must have been about this time, or even a year later, that Aunt Kate wrote to me at Easter, telling me to try and think of myself as Mary Magdalene (who brought spices to the tomb on Easter Day). It was the kind of letter that always embarrassed me; I left it on the bathroom mantelpiece, and went to bed. Here Christopher found and read it. The next morning he remarked: 'I hope you feel complimented.'

'Complimented? What by?'

'Well – Mary Magdalene.'

'What is the mystery?' One knew there was one. She was sometimes identified as the woman from whom seven devils were cast out.

'You know.'

'I don't. Tell me. I feel so silly not knowing.'

'Well.' Christopher hesitated. Then: 'She was a harlot.'

'Oh! I thought that was a vegetable.'

'You're thinking of a shallot.'

'So I am. What's the other thing you said?'

'You'd better look it up in a dictionary.'

So I found the dictionary and proceeded patiently from harlot to strumpet, and strumpet to whore and still felt horribly puzzled.

'I don't see the use of dictionaries,' I said pettishly, 'if they can't make you understand perfectly simple things.'

When I was older I recognised the story of Mary Magdalene as among the most magnificent of the many magnificent stories of the early Christian Church. For moral courage I have never met any to surpass it. But I knew nothing about that, then. Only I felt vaguely discomfited.

The following year I sat for my Junior Scholarship.

'You realise that if you want your education to continue, you must be successful,' said my father gravely.

I nodded with comprehension. Naturally, I had. When I heard that one of the scholarships had been awarded to me I knew my education was safe until I was sixteen.

Nowadays I am hard put to it to remember anything I learnt during the next three years that was the slightest use to me once I had left school. I had a smattering of every subject, including Greek, but no sound unified knowledge of any one of them. The trouble was there seemed to be no sense of continuity in the curriculum. In history, for example, you might 'do' the Plantagenets one year, the Tudors the next, and the following year go back to Gustavus Adolphus, the Lion of the North. There was no idea of teaching European history contemporaneously, or suggesting that the events in one country had inevitable bearing on the behaviour of another.

This was quite a general attitude at that time. Martin Boyd in his autobiography confesses that he was overwhelmed with shame when, as a boy, he was asked his favourite character in French history, because he had thought all history was English. You never thought of the world as a commonwealth of nations, all interdependent, all contributing something to a common fund. There was England – i.e. the Empire – and there was the rest of the world. Naturally, all the views expressed must be intensely patriotic. A girl who felt sympathy for any other country in one of England's many wars was sent to Coventry. We seriously didn't think she should be allowed to remain and contaminate the school. It was the same with literature. Literature was essentially

English. That there might be a French, a German, a
Russian literature never occurred to us. There were one
or two French playwrights who were studied by the
French VIIth, but that was all. Geography was a matter
of European capitals and principal imports and exports;
also of drawing maps with furry lines for the mountain
ranges. In arithmetic we did logarithms and surds, but
were never taught to keep accounts or take out a balance,
things we might conceivably have to do later on. As for
the history of our times, anything we learnt about that
we learnt at home. We could tell you the date when King
John signed Magna Charta, and discuss the 'reforms' of
the Protectorate, but we knew nothing of Robert Owen
or any of the reformers of the past century. Industrial
history was never so much as mentioned, and we had no
sense of the links binding the various classes of the community. Worst of all, it was never put to us that, because
of what other Englishmen had done in the past, we were
what we were today (except, of course, that if it hadn't
been for the Protestant Reformation we should all still
be under the heel of the Roman Church), or that we
were the historians of our own time, and that what we
achieved would direct and determine the lives of those
who followed after us.

By fifteen, at latest, youth should have some under-
standing of the nature of corporate responsibility. The
nearest we got to it was 'team spirit' on the playing-fields.
All our French lessons were woefully alike, and quite
uninspired. *Chardenal's Grammar, Bué's Exercises, La Mère*

Michel et son Chat, Tartarin de Tarascon, and so forth. We never had even one half-hour a week set aside during which we tried to talk in French and in French only. We knew nothing of French conversation.

'Avez-vous la plume de ma tante?'

'Non, mais j'ai le chapeau de votre oncle.'

We didn't think of the French as human beings, like ourselves, separated by a strip of water and a foreign language, both barriers very easy to overcome. Frenchmen were foreigners, Germans were foreigners, Russians were foreigners, though these last were so far removed from the British mentality as hardly to count as human beings at all.

And what remains of the Latin one learned then?

> *Common are to either sex*
> *Artifex and opifex.*

And

> *Amo, amas*
> *I loved a lass,*
> *And she was tall and slender.*
> *Amas, amat,*
> *She knocked me flat*
> *Over the feminine gender.*

English literature began with the *Canterbury Tales* and ended with Browning. No one who wasn't dead could be literature. There were Francis Thompson, Swinburne,

Alice Meynell – but Thompson took drugs, Swinburne was erotic, Alice Meynell a Catholic.

Perhaps the main charge I should like to bring against education as I knew it is a complete absence of stimulus to the individual. If you were 'booky' or a 'swot', and of course if you were going to be a schoolmarm, you worked hard; but there was as a rule a feeling that school was simply something to be got through, something that could be quite fun while it lasted, but not an important introduction to the future, no sense, indeed, of the future being here and now. It was like the religious teaching of the period. You tried to live a good life in order to be fitted for eternity; and hardly anybody seemed to think that eternity is also here and now, that it begins in this world, and that this life is simply its first chapter, without which the entire story would be unintelligible.

We weren't taught to be speculative, controversial, to consider other possible angles of belief. No, the rich man was in his castle and the poor man at his gate because, mysteriously, God had willed it so, and that the rich man might have obtained his position by graft and the poor man sunk through drink or be the victim of social injustice was never offered as a conceivable alternative. Indeed, all through my school years I never once heard the word 'economics'. In winter we all huddled round the fire, and if the price of coal went up householders complained, but we knew nothing of the miner's way of life, or felt any responsibility for social conditions. It did not even seem to us that the majority of grown-up people felt any such responsibility. A whole world of speculation and knowledge that should have been ours was never opened to us.

I daresay a few of the more enterprising discovered it for themselves. I remembered at about fourteen finding Mrs Gaskell's *Mary Barton* in the school library, and being horrified at the description of the lives of mill operatives and the appalling conditions under which they worked. I demanded excitedly if it were true.

'That wasn't in our time. Things aren't like that now.'

And yet on that very day there must have been women working in the factories for seven-and-six a week. My own grandmother had employed a sempster to make her nightgowns by hand – and what tucks and frills and feather-stitching they expected then. She paid her three-and-sixpence and her meals – that is her midday dinner and tea. A nightgown, if you worked like a fury, could be made in two days, though generally you had to work late at your own house. Working six days a week you might earn half a guinea.

I burned with indignation when I heard this.

'It's wicked,' I protested.

'If they didn't complain, and they never did, you may be sure they were satisfied.'

And not so long afterwards I heard of women working at the needle for a penny an hour all the year round.

Presumably some of the clothes we wore, wonderful bargains they were called, were the fruits of sweated labour. But we knew nothing of such conditions, weren't encouraged to inquire into them, any more than we were encouraged to visit the slums that flourished all over the country. We were – I see it now – like children in a fairy-tale. We knew nothing at all about real life.

Nor can I remember any preceptress raising the question of: What do you intend to be? And what are you doing about building the foundations? For sixteen isn't a child; it's a potential adult who should already be thinking of the part that will be his share in the communal life.

Of course, there were Suffragettes, wild women who chained themselves to railings and had to be forcibly fed. Naturally, none of our aunts belonged to that crowd.

'But why do they do it?'

'Because they want a vote.'

'Why do they want a vote?'

'To show they're as good as men.'

'And aren't they?'

An awkward question, that. 'It isn't a question of being as good. It's being different.'

Still, if a large proportion of the country were women, wasn't it logical they should have some say in its government?

'Any woman worth her salt can persuade at least one man to vote as she wants,' said the cynical sophisticated.

Even that didn't sound very satisfactory. Rulers who could be swayed, possibly against their own inclinations, by personal considerations, were hardly the rulers in whom one would have much faith. And if women had so much power and could thus vote indirectly, why not give them the vote direct?

'Women don't know enough.'

'Couldn't they learn?'

'Hadn't you better finish your Latin preparation?'

After all, in 1913 marriage was still supposed to be woman's ultimate goal. There were even men who still disputed a married woman's right to her own property, although, under law, it had been at her own disposal for years now.

'Women don't understand money. If they give their attention to looking after their houses and bringing up their children, that should occupy all their time. Men don't interfere in their sphere, why should they interfere in a man's?'

As for the women who didn't contrive a husband, they were presumably beneath contempt. An unmarried son was some one to be proud of, but an unmarried daughter was a reproach. And even the married women, for all this line of argument so glibly asserted, didn't really bring up their children. They had nurses for them from the first month, and then governesses, and when they were older, the really difficult age, they packed them off to school. Nor did they run their own houses. They gave a few orders to servants who did all the real work; and perhaps they 'did the flowers'. One wonders – what on earth did mothers and aunts do all day in the time before the war?

'They had a b—— awful time,' an elderly man confessed to me, 'especially if they lived in the country. Once a week they might join a class that learnt to paint on china, which, as a rule, meant spoiling perfectly good plates. And there was needlework – and the Sunday School – and making garments for the heathen ...'

'Suppose you were the kind that didn't believe in trying to convert the heathen?'

But, apparently, if you were one of those you were *anathema maranatha* and cast into outer (social) darkness.

How one tried to fathom this mystery. 'Mother, why should some people be born to employ servants and others to be them?'

'Things have always been like that.'

That was the blind alley in which one always ended.

'Why should houses have to be arranged to suit men? Why should boys have more pocket money than girls and stay up later, even when the girls are older?'

'Because they're going to be men. They'll have to work.'

It seemed clear that, having made the initial mistake of being born a woman, if anything was to be done about the future, it would have to be done through one's own efforts, and there was no time to lose. After all, not only men, but I, too, would have a living to earn. Of course, there was marriage, but it seemed tacitly accepted that that was an improbability in this case. So there remained work.

What work?

Adults had it all planned out. 'If you do well at school and get a senior scholarship (as of course you will), you can then proceed to the University. Naturally, you will have to be Very Careful. As soon as you have taken a degree you will Get a Position. Then you begin to pay into a superannuation fund. If you never let your payments lapse, by the time you are due to retire, say sixty-five or so, you will have earned a pension, and whatever happens you will never actually starve.'

'But – I don't want to be a school teacher. They have awful lives. Nobody ever likes them, not really.'

'It is Very Useful Work.' And, of course, the kind of work a Lady Could Do.

'I mean to be a writer.'

'That will be very nice for your spare time.'

'I meant – all the time.'

'Have you forgotten – you have to earn a living?'

'But there have been writers – there was Shakespeare ...' No, perhaps better to skate hurriedly over Shakespeare. 'And Charles Dickens. And George Eliot. And Sir Walter Scott.'

'Of course, if you think you are the equal of any of those ...'

'Well, actually, I don't, but I don't see why you should be so sure. I might be.' And at that time I had a sneaking feeling that perhaps, after all, I am.

It's tiresome that no one seems to take your idea about writing as a career seriously. It is obvious that something must be done. The day of the Correspondence College was in its infancy, but some pioneer (was it Sir

Max Pemberton?) was blazing the trail to be followed by hundreds in after years, many of them incompetent, some of them sheer rogues. Sir Max (assuming it was Sir Max) has collected an army of men, prominent men, journalists and editors, with a publisher thrown in for luck, and these have combined in producing a booklet called *Writing for the Press*. A couple of stamps will bring the book to your door. After that, you simply have to keep a wary look-out for the postman.

That booklet would fill the most timid with hope. Every One Can Write. If you have a Gift, so much the better. But in any case, don't let your friends discourage you. If you can write a good letter, you can write for the Press. There's no reason, these experts insist, why writing shouldn't be a paying career, a good deal more paying than school-marming. Editors are clamouring for new authors; new authors are clamouring for a hearing. The trouble is that up to date no one has been on hand to advise them how to make their work marketable. Writing is like everything else – it needs training. A man doesn't expect his first painting to be accepted by the Academy, but every one has the idea that he can write. Before Sir Max had this brilliant notion of education through the post, unfortunate would-be writers slithered in a morass of ignorance and disappointment. Often they gave up altogether, for want of a helping hand and a guiding light. This Correspondence Course was the Short Cut to Success – and you could have it for ten pounds.

Father stood on the hearth-rug, warming his coat-tails.

To him entered his elder daughter, one hand carefully concealed behind her back.

'Oh, Father, I've been thinking – about the future, I mean – if you could let me have ten pounds I could take this course, and as it only lasts six months and you earn while you learn, by the time I'm fifteen I'd be helping you to pay the rent. Wouldn't that be grand?'

Father has that magnificent simplicity that is, we understand, impossible to the tortuous female mind.

'It might be,' he agrees, 'but I haven't got ten pounds.'

'Perhaps we could pay in instalments. Two pounds to start with and then so much a month. If you could give me two pounds ...'

'And what about the subsequent instalments?'

'Oh, you earn while you learn. I should have enough by the time the next instalment was due.'

Men – the majority of them – in this year of grace before the Great War – had no particular regard for female intellect, particularly when it was arrayed in gym tunic and plaits.

'What's that thing you've got hold of?'

'It's called *Writing for the Press*. It's ...'

Father waves it away. 'Write! Under my roof! Never!'

When you have lived for more than fourteen years with a person it is hard to be taken by surprise. Obviously you must construct some alternative plan. Up in the attic bedroom, a huge barn of a place, you think – and think. It is clear that *Writing for the Press* must wait for the moment. Meanwhile, may it not be that there are exceptions to the rule that you Must Be Trained before you can sell? The great essential is a typewriter. Hand-written work is the hall-mark of the amateur. Clearly you can't buy a typewriter or even hire one, but there's a place called Pitman's College where girls take courses in typewriting and shorthand. It might be as well to inquire further.

Two more stamps, a little more vigilance in the hall, and you can pore to your heart's content over a gener-ously illustrated prospectus, with pictures of sensible-looking girls in white shirts and bootlace ties pounding on divine typewriters. The next step was less simple. After all, the scholarship provided another two years at St Bride's. There were evening classes, but you couldn't attend those without confiding in your family, and they would cost money ... One had to reflect.

These reflections were brought to an abrupt head the following Saturday morning by the unanticipated appearance of a young man in a raincoat and bowler hat, carrying a leather case, who pushed open the gate, rang the bell and asked for me by name. My mother and I were standing by the dining-room window and got a full view of the arrival.

'What is that common-looking young man doing coming up my steps?' wondered my mother.

Then the maid came in, carrying a card, that she handed to me.

'Gentleman for Miss Lucy.'

'And what,' inquired my mother glacially, 'does this mean?'

Stammering, crimson, furious at this development, I was driven to explanations.

'And how do you propose to deal with that – person?'

'Couldn't you see him and just explain that I'm still at school and I've got a scholarship, and of course I won't be leaving yet, so it's no good——'

'Certainly not,' said my mother. 'You got him into the house. You can get him out.'

Knees shaking, an awkward hobbledehoy in a dark blue cotton blouse with a detachable collar almost permanently detached, black ribbed stockings, clumping black shoes, as plain as they're made and well aware of it, further disfigured by steel-rimmed glasses, I forced myself to enter the drawing-room. The young man stood patiently looking at nothing. His face, when he saw me, betrayed nothing at all.

Nervously I apologised for bringing him on a fool's errand.

'You see, I wouldn't be leaving school yet…'

He was unexpectedly helpful; said he quite understood, that his people never wanted to hustle possible clients; but perhaps I'd keep the brochure…

I promised I would and out he went. But after that it seemed advisable to emulate Brer Rabbit for a bit. Besides, there was some talk about clandestine correspondence, which sounded as though it ought to be more interesting than, actually, it was.

★

So I shelved my ambitions and continued sending verses to the Competition Pages of *Little Folks* and worked in a desultory sort of way for the senior scholarship examination for which I should have to sit in the summer of 1914. It had suddenly become apparent to me that, though I didn't intend to become a schoolmarm, I definitely didn't want to leave school yet. But the dice were too heavily loaded against me. To begin with, I didn't really work hard enough, and for another thing, I had not contrived to impress the authorities with the fact that I was of the stuff of whom scholarship girls should be made. No matter what good intentions accompanied me at the beginning of term, before six weeks were up I was riding on an uncommonly bumpy track.

If you are extremely shy and equally ambitious, and take great pains to conceal your shyness and none to conceal your ambition, the sum total is not going to appeal to those in authority. The artificial aggressiveness that comes from bashfulness and the genuine aggressiveness that comes from a firm belief that you are born to be one of the lights of your generation, combine to produce a pretty unsatisfactory total. So, at least, my head mistress considered, and I daresay plenty of others agreed with her.

Well, there it was. When the results came through, I was not on the list of successes. For two days I cried as though my heart would burst. I remember sitting on the curly tapestry sofa in the drawing-room and envying passionately all those who have died young. Of course the gods loved them – and equally of course, not even the gods loved me. I knew then that Hamlet was wrong when he said it was better to bear the ills one had than fly to those one knew not of. At least those had the advantage of novelty. Meanwhile, here was I, with my life in ruins, all through my own fault, my own laziness, my own unattractive temperament. I was like the man who buried his talent and was condemned therefor.

I thought about suicide, not with intent to accomplish it; I knew suicide was the unforgivable sin, since it allowed no space for repentance. But could it be wrong to wish for one of those swift and painless illnesses that achieved the same effect?

Rootling in one of the attics I came upon a book of verses, entitled *Spring, Summer and Autumn Leaves*, and therein a poem:

> *Fate gives us all one chance, they say,*
> *She gave me mine that November day,*
> *She gave me mine and I threw it away.*

Yes, I'd had mine and I'd let it slip; it wouldn't come again. All my life I should regret my folly. From my obscurity I should perceive the honourable career that might have been mine. In short, I should be, to my dying hour, the victim of an Irremediable Remorse.

But within about a fortnight even my ruined life seemed comparatively unimportant, for on the 4th of August Britain went to war.

Chapter Four

I remember that morning. It was a Sunday and I, since I was now confirmed, had been to the Early Service with my father. When we came out of church he did a thing I had never known him do before. He bought a Sunday paper. We were not even supposed to take buses on Sunday or spend any money at all, except in the church plate. Standing in the middle of the road where two sets of tramlines intersected, he opened the paper. Then he said, in a voice I did not know: 'Thank God, we've declared war.'

A policeman crossed the street and touched him on the arm. 'Excuse me, sir. That tram would like to pass.'

Things happened very quickly; the eldest of my naval cousins, who usually spent their holidays with us, was recalled to his ship; the second one, who was not quite fifteen, never joined us at all. Then I heard that a third cousin, a young civil engineer, had joined the army as a private. It was then that the war became a personal reality, as apart from a general national upheaval.

The Stock Exchange closed down at once. This was desperately serious for us.

My mother said: 'I can't think what we shall do. We shall have no money, not any servants even. We shall have to do our own work.'

I said: 'Do you mean you will have to open doors to tradesmen?' and she replied: 'We will hope it doesn't come to that.'

Stockbrokers and jobbers were left absolutely high and dry. Many of them, like my father, had young children – too young to earn – and little, if anything, in the way of savings. They applied everywhere for possible work, for the duration of the war, although at that time a lot of people thought Horatio Bottomley was right, and that the war would be over by Christmas. My father applied with the rest. He would bicycle up to London from St Leonards, and bicycle back again. Already the roads were lined with sentries, only too apt to let off a rifle at once if a challenge was not instantly responded to.

The rumour went round that the country was honey-combed with spies, and my mother said she was thankful that some sixth sense had made her send a telegram to the German governess she had actually engaged the previous month.

Father was a practised cyclist but already pretty deaf; we were never happy about him during those first weeks of the war until we got his card from London, saying he had arrived safely.

He was one of the comparatively lucky ones. After some anxious weeks he was appointed to the Records Office at Woolwich. This meant he could live at home and go to his office daily. He left very early in the morning and travelled a good part of the way by tram; we used to come down and supervise his breakfast, for our household staff was reduced to French Marie, who did not sleep in, and did not care about cooking or coming early.

Meanwhile the war had proved only the first of two bad shocks I had that summer, and for a time, at least, the second seemed the worse of the two. This was my chance discovery of something menacing the whole social structure, a thing called The White Slave Traffic. In the house my mother had taken furnished, there was very little to read. I had, of course, no money to buy books or to borrow them. But read I must. I was driven to devouring the columns of the newspaper sheets lining the dressing-table drawers; I read, until I knew it almost by heart, the inquest on a man who had deliberately run his car into a bank to save two carters.

'He died for the likes of we,' one of the survivors was reported as saying. I thought it was the most pathetic thing I had ever heard.

On another sheet I found a copy of Fred Weatherly's 'Friend O' Mine' (or am I confusing this with the house in Steyning where Father and I went in the summer of 1917: I read newspaper columns there, also). Anyhow, I thought it so beautiful that later on I copied it into my commonplace book. And then, one day, hunting for something fresh, I unearthed, from the top of the wardrobe, a paper-covered book on The Traffic. It filled me with a terror only equivalent to my original terror of hell. It was a disaster from which even extreme caution could not necessarily save you. You might answer an advertisement – and how did you get jobs else? – or you might be asked by a fainting woman to accompany her home in a taxi – and at once your fate was sealed.

The book was juicy with detail. Many of the victims were shipped to South America, at once; some were sent to Paris. I supposed that, if ever I were caught, since my French was atrocious, they would hardly send me there. But quite a number remained in London, worked like dogs by their 'bullies', starved and beaten if they failed to 'bring home' sufficient money. On the other hand, if they did well they were bought nice frocks and taken care of. I was quite hazy as to what was demanded of these unfortunates, but I supposed that what other women did could also be achieved by me.

Then I would look in the glass and say hopefully, 'They wouldn't want any one as plain as that,' but a further glance at the book reminded me that women of all types were abducted and shanghaied. Even the war seemed a less immediate fear than this. I wondered whether you ever got used to the life, if you ever escaped, and, if so, if you could ever return to decent society. It seemed to me there was no security left anywhere in the world.

For years afterwards it haunted me, becoming particularly vivid whenever I applied for a new job. But I felt this was a subject that could be mentioned to no one. I must keep it, like a viper, to bite my own bosom.

Back at school the change in the world was instantly apparent. A number of familiar faces had disappeared. Mine was not the only father who had been hard hit by the war. Others found they could not pay even the moderate fees that the foundation demanded and removed their daughters, notice being waived in the circumstances. In the Junior School one saw numbers of patriotic rosettes, tiny medallions of Lord Kitchener or the King or Admiral Jellicoe, set in the heart of yards of narrow red, white, and blue ribbon. There was, too, a new portrait in the hall of Princess Mary, done in colours. The head mistress called a grand meeting of the whole school in the big hall, and told us that every time we passed that picture we must remember that it represented the ideal of British womanhood.

We were to remember, also, that although we were for the most part too young to take any active part in the war, we could think of ourselves as part of a great army fighting for righteousness. She was going to propose that each class thought of itself as a regiment, and of its form-mistress as its superior officer. Girls in uniform – i.e. in gym tunics – were to salute any mistress they met in the hall or corridors; girls in undress would curtsey. Also we were each to choose a form motto and a form 'tune' to be played during the monthly reviews she purposed holding. We must not, of course, choose the National Anthem of any allied country. We should not like it if any other country allowed its schoolgirls to choose as their marching tune God Save the King.

There was a murmur behind me, swiftly suppressed: 'Gosh, think of trying to march to that.'

We were also told that at such a time we should be especially courteous to those who, through no fault of their own, found themselves of alien, if not actually enemy, nationality in the land where they were now living. We had among us one such who had a special claim upon our consideration. This was the German mistress, a dark swarthy little woman with a wild frizz of hair, known colloquially as Froggy.

There was a seethe of conversation as soon as we were released. The juniors thought it might all be rather fun, but the older girls were dubious from the start. The VIIIth wore skirts to their heels and had their hair up, not just in a door-knocker but really 'up'. It was difficult to think of them curtseying every time a mistress passed. We wore gym dresses most of the time, and we supposed we could learn to salute without giggling, but curtseys were a different affair. Our skirts were short and not very wide; we should look such fools. Down in the playroom in the basement we got together, when there were no seniors about, and practised.

Poor Froggy! It was an unhappy situation for her. She didn't have a very easy time. Which ever way you looked at it, we argued, she was a traitor. If she was a good German she ought to back her own country in every circumstance, even when they were as flagrantly wrong as they were now; if she didn't she was a traitor to them, and if she was loyal she would probably be asked to become a spy, and we wanted no spies in our English school. I don't think she lasted the war. It was too difficult. Besides, parents had their suspicions. People were very hard on men and women with German names just then. One old man who had been resident in England for fifty years had his windows broken and foul threats shouted from the streets, until neither he nor his wife dared go out. That was in the East End. Some even were haled to internment camps. The father of one of Christopher's schoolmates was referred to as a spy, and came into the courts on that account. When he showed that he had a son serving with the British forces and had himself been resident in England most of his life, he won his case with heavy damages.

Our school reviews did not last long. They were held – I think – each month. The procedure was as follows. Each form in turn, beginning with the lowest form of the lower school, paraded round the great hall to its chosen tune, played from the platform by the music mistress. Then they were drawn up in a semi-circle, and the form-mistress – we wondered if we ought to address them as lieutenant or captain, but this was not encouraged – read out the names of those who were commended, either

71

for school work or for moral qualities. For instance, a girl who had broken her arm playing hockey and had displayed unusual courage when it was set, was commended; and any girl who had won 'A' for the week was commended, and stepped out of the ranks when her name was called. I once got 'A' and stood out in my turn, but I noticed that all my companions looked like nervous horses about to shy. Quite soon these reviews came to an end. I suppose the upper forms objected. After all, they were old enough to have brothers in France, and after the first Christmas the sight of a girl in dead mourning became quite common. We stuck to our mottoes, however. As I was on the classical side, ours was in Latin: *Altiora peto* – I seek higher things.

One quickly got accustomed to the fact of war. Food became very dear, potatoes were scarce, you bought margarine instead of butter, and shoes were made of synthetic leather that was mainly cardboard. We had practice drills at school, rushing out at the tolling of a bell, only to find the school porter at the foot of the staircase waving a flaming branch, and a mistress calling, 'You can't get out this way.' So back we would go and along the corridor and down the other staircase. We had sudden black-outs, too; I never saw a black-out during the war, except at school. And we put up blue blinds at the windows, because of the new regulation about showing lights.

Everybody knitted; I tried, with the rest, but with

a complete lack of success; eventually I bought some unbleached calico and started to make casualty bags. These were completed with a drawstring and a label; when a man was brought into a casualty clearing station all his possessions were dumped into this bag, his name was written on the label, and they were kept for him if he recovered, and for his relatives, if he did not. I made four, but the labels presented difficulties. Wherever a needle went in it made a hole; and the labels themselves would get dirty. So eventually I kept mine (there were only four) to send handkerchiefs to the laundry at home.

A tremendous patriotic wave overflowed and drenched most of us to the skin. I cut out photographs of the B.E.F. and pinned them to the sloping walls of my room. I had photographs of Admiral Jellicoe, Lord Beatty, and Sir Reginald Tyrwhitt on the wall over the fireplace, and in my dreams I would meet them, and become involved in mysterious secret service raids. No one ever suspected the plain spectacled schoolgirl; but after I left school the following year I abandoned these follies.

We went to church, as usual, and heard astounding sermons; nowadays I suppose they could hardly be preached. One man said, 'Christ prayed for His murderers for they knew not what they did, but He never commanded us to pray for our enemies who know the atrocity of their sin.' That was during the rape of Belgium. The Bishop of London gave his famous address on the Nailed as opposed to the Mailed Hand, but most people, including the clergy, forgot that that hand was nailed – to a

Cross. It was not until some time after peace had been signed that Dean Inge wrote that the only command laid upon this nation during the war years was to pray for its enemies, but in 1914 that attitude was unheard of. After some time we had to give up going to church on Sunday nights, for the streets were so dark, and the church (as usual) so far away, that it became nervous work walking there and back. All manner of queer folk were lurking in London, so we read the psalms and lessons at home.

The war was not over by Christmas, as so many people had predicted; indeed, it began to look as though it might be a long affair. Those of one's aunts who were suitable were nursing; nobody thought it was proper to write novels and one was a little ashamed of reading them.

I was still, despite the war, unresigned to the thought of leaving school. At Christmas it seemed to me that if I saved all my tips, and added to them any further tips that might come my way – I had a birthday in February – Providence in some guise or another would miraculously make up the deficit. So that year I would not go to theatres or pictures or even buy a book. I stored my money away, added a little more in February and waited hopefully for faith to be justified. In this case, however, it never was, and when it became clear that I should be leaving in July my mother suggested I might like to spend the money buying myself some clothes. I bought a double-decker skirt for ten shillings, which seemed to me a lot of money, and was mildly disappointed that it attracted no outward admiration when I wore it at school. I bought some heavy cotton blouses with detachable collars and a pair of shoes.

That year I entered for the Essay Prize. The subject was a quotation from Shakespeare.

The poet's eye, in a fine frenzy rolling,
Doth glance from heaven to earth, from earth to heaven,
And as imagination bodies forth
The forms of things unknown, the poet's pen
Turns them to shapes and gives to airy nothing
A local habitation and a name.

I used to sit in the school library through long sunny afternoons that last term, with piles of books round me, culling suitable quotations, surrounded by contemporaries all doing the same thing. When I was in the Lower School I always had 'Quotations Good' scrawled in blue chalk in the margin. Things were simpler in those days. When I could recall no classical quotation that seemed to hit the mark, I quoted recklessly from Ethel M. Dell, whose stories appeared in the *Red Magazine*. Thus, in an essay concerning death – though I can't think why – I wrote, 'As a brave man has said, death is only the opening and shutting of a door.' If we had had to give contexts I should have had to quote her latest success, *The Keeper of the Door*. It didn't, at that time, occur to me that any one might have said this before Miss Dell. When even she failed me, I would invent apt quotations, either in prose or verse, enclose them in the appropriate inverted commas, and the result was always 'Excellent'. But I felt for this competition such a method was too dangerous. So I sat studying for hours...

I might have saved myself the trouble. I was not even *proxime accessit*.

End of term came much too soon. I had no plans. It no longer seemed likely that I was about to burst in the glory of genius on an astonished world. Anyway, the war had changed everything. I lined up with all the other leaving girls outside the head mistress's study, clutching the red leather prayer-book I had been given four and a half years ago, when I arrived. It had to have the date of my leaving in it, and then it became my own property. Where is it now, with its stamped design of laurel leaves and its gold monogram on the cover? I had it for years, but I lost it when I came to Edwardes Square.

I cried for days after leaving school, and felt I had been shabbily treated by a world that didn't care a damn what happened to me. For some time I tried to keep up my studies. I bought long blue exercise books at Straker's, and mapped out my time into half-hours – Greek, Latin, mathematics, French, German (I even tried to learn this) – but there was no encouragement, it was too late to hope to pass exams or take degrees, there was a lot to be done at home, silver and brass to be polished, shopping, bedmaking, dusting; one learned to help in the kitchen, even (with a disgust that seems queer now) to wash dishes.

Then in November I had a belated summer holiday with some near-relatives. I liked them because, instead of good advice, they gave me a skirt that I needed much more. It was made of serviceable grey tweed and was put together by the family dressmaker. She was a little woman with a poking head, who lived in a side-street away from the sea. My eldest 'aunt' took me up, still wearing the two-decker skirt, and said: 'Oh, Miss Blank, I want you to make a skirt for my niece. Make it on the pattern you used for that skirt of Miss Florrie's last month.'

Miss Florrie was the second of the sisters and must have been well over forty at this time. The skirt was very long and had a kind of little dip at the back, like a curtailed train, but I was very proud of it notwithstanding. It was the first time I had ever had anything made for me.

They asked me what I meant to do, and I said, learn shorthand and typewriting if I get the chance. After I came back to London they wrote, offering me a six-weeks' course at a commercial college, but my pride was still sufficiently unbroken for me to say, I think I should like something better than that. In spite of my haughtiness they sent me the coat that matched the skirt when Christmas came round. It had a broad belt and a black velvet collar, and was lined with blue and white shirting. Then, while we were still discussing my future, my other godmother wrote from out of the blue, to say that she had arranged for me to learn secretarial work at a private school that had been recommended by a great friend, who now had a position on *The Times*. I still had a few shillings of my savings left, and I bought a black velveteen pork-pie hat, mounted on cardboard, though I did not know this at the time, and woollen gloves, and the family gave me an attaché case.

The day before I was to begin Mother took me to Victoria Street and we walked up and down looking at the outside of the buildings. But in spite of this, I was so stupid that the next morning I left the train at Victoria instead of proceeding to St James's Park. All the troop trains left from Victoria and it was associated in my mind with the end of the civilised world.

Chapter Five

Term had started a week before my arrival, and everyone knew the shorthand alphabet and was doing short sentences. It was like a return to the nursery. 'The fat cat sat on the mat' would have been far beyond the pretensions of any of us, for we knew nothing as yet of the halving principle to indicate 't' where no vowel follows. There were about a dozen of us in my class, the eldest a woman who would never see forty again, the youngest about a year or eighteen months older than myself. I thought that, after all, life had given me one more chance and this time I would not let it slip.

It was a new thing to me to have an allowance to handle. Not a dress allowance, of course, but a Luncheon-and-Tea Fund. This began at half a crown a week, and as tea was a compulsory ninepence, that left me 1s. 9d. for five meals and any incidental expenses that might crop up. At first I went to Lyons and alternated between a cup of soup and a roll (4d.) and a glass of milk with a dash (2½d.) and an unbuttered scone (1d.). I looked forward to the days when I should be independent and have steak and kidney pudding (7d.) and fried potatoes (2½d.), like the established clerks and typists I met there. I never had this meal all through my training, and later I was told by a woman with twenty-five years' experience of wage-earning that she had spent 5d. a day for the past twelve years. She always had the same lunch – the pudding of the day (3d.) and two penny buns. When she got back to the office she drank a glass of water. After a little I persuaded my mother to give me half a crown in addition to the ninepence for tea, for I soon discovered there were various essentials I must acquire. The first of these was a fountain pen. We were told (erroneously, I think) that we should always find it simpler to read back our shorthand outlines if we made them with a pen rather than a pencil. Actually, I have never seen any one use a pen for reporting. A Blackbird, the cheapest reliable pen on the market, cost five shillings, and it was an easy matter to go without lunch altogether for two weeks and on the following Monday turn up triumphantly with a pen, like everybody else. Then there was the question of a watch. As I did not lunch, I would go either to the Park or to Westminster Abbey during my lunch-hour. I got to know the Poets' Corner by heart, and I spent a lot of time in St Faith's Chapel, too, for I was beginning to be troubled about the numbers of men at the front for whom, I thought, there might be no one to pray. So I used to go to this little chapel to pray for them. Our lunch-time was limited to one hour sharp, and I always came back much too soon, peering into teashops to catch a glimpse of the time. And when I had a job, I thought I should probably lose it the next morning if I turned up late. So, after the pen, I bought a watch.

Messrs. Samuel on Westminster Bridge put grand-looking watches in the window, priced seven-and-six-pence, so for three weeks I kept my lunch money and on the third Friday I walked through the doors and asked for a watch. The assistant who served me brought some out, adding that, although these were wonderful value for money, if I could pay a little more I would get a much better bargain. I began to panic.

'How much more?'

'We have an amazing watch for ten shillings.'

I carried my money in a little Dorothy purse. I now turned this upside down on the counter, so that the three half-crowns rolled out.

'That is all I have,' I said.

'You might leave this as a deposit, and when you bring us the last half-crown you could take the watch. We would keep it for you until then.'

'I could bring you the money on Monday,' I said earnestly, 'but I must take the watch home tonight.'

He gave it to me – without asking for my name or address he gave it to me – and on Monday I rushed into the shop and discharged my debt. That watch went a good deal better than many a more expensive one I have had since.

★

The Army and Navy Stores were a great source of entertainment on lunchless days. This was before they rebuilt
their book department. This was an ideal haunt for a
'snitcher'. You found a book you wanted, you carried
it away behind the section marked 'Theological Works'
where hardly anybody came and, standing first on one
foot and then on the other, you could read as much as
two chapters before it was time to return to the office.
The assistants were charming. They never tried to sell
you anything or stood about in suspicious attitudes, star-
ing. If my book was particularly absorbing I would bury
it behind a row of theological works as neatly as a dog
interring a bone, and would rediscover it nonchalantly
the next day. Sometimes I would stay away from the
stores for two days together; I feared I might be making
myself conspicuous.

I generally lunched off a penny bun or a bar of chocolate, for Pitman's published various books in shorthand
– some of the stories of Sherlock Holmes, I remember,
and (I think) *The Sign of Four*, as well as regular weekly
papers; I bought all these and also a shorthand dictionary.
But after a time I only went out for a quarter of an
hour, just to deceive the others, and would then come
slipping back to the empty office, where, on the heavy
old-fashioned non-visible machines that were provided
for the learners, I would type out original verses that I
sent faithfully to papers all over London.

About this time someone told me that W. L. George
once papered a room with rejection slips, and I reflected,

somewhat consoled, that so far I couldn't even paper a cupboard with mine. All the same, these persistent rebuffs worried me. I had tried two or three short stories, but they had all been returned. It seemed to me time was rushing on and I had so far nothing to show for my life. I was seventeen, and I agreed with the childish heroine who, told that she had all her life before her, retorted that a good deal of it already lay behind. On Sundays I would look at the rows of devout women, each of whom, doubtless, had her crown laid up for her in Heaven, and reflect that I could hardly expect similar recognition. I wanted to achieve something very quickly, to reassure myself I hadn't wasted my life.

So I sat up in bed at night practising touch typewriting on a model keyboard, whose keys, once depressed, seldom rose again, and I took down sermons in shorthand and afterwards transcribed them faithfully, and learnt all the special abbreviations at the back of the Shorthand Instructor; and I never thought of going to a theatre or having a pot of face cream or a box of powder or art-silk stockings or shoes with high heels or an evening frock. I was still young enough to feel there was something rather shocking about enjoying a war, as quite obviously a lot of people, particularly women, were doing. When my class-mates remonstrated with me for working overtime and getting ahead – I was by this time two chapters in front of any one – I told them earnestly, 'But this is my chance – don't you see?' No, it wasn't surprising that I made no friends at my training school.

★

That was the summer of 1916. Christopher – who hadn't flunked his senior scholarship – left school and went to a training camp at Oxford; afterwards he became a cadet officer and went out to France in the Tank Corps.

Towards the end of our training Miss G. would send us out in response to enquiries for a clerk or a typist, to give us practice. I used to wonder if she charged as much for us as she did for her experts; we were all inexperienced and slow and didn't really know the layout of much of the work we were given. My first job was to an elderly Jew called Zimmerman who had an office in Victoria Street. As soon as Miss G. told me about him all my dread of the White Slave Traffic returned to me. I choked. I said, 'Oh yes. You want me to go?'

She said keenly, 'Certainly. You can go at once,' and then she added, 'If you want to hold responsible positions, it is very important always to be as neat as a new pin.'

I flushed guiltily. I had put up my hair to come to this place; it was straight and unadaptable; even the infallible tape tie did nothing to help me. Miss G. produced the largest safety-pin I have ever seen.

'If your skirt has a tendency to drag' (it had, of course; it weighed a ton, and in those days we wore blouses with tape ties on them that showed if the skirt slipped a fraction of an inch) 'you may find this useful.'

I thought she might have waited until we were alone in the room.

I jammed on my hat, took my notebook and a pencil,

and went out. Mr Zimmerman's office was at the end of a short corridor, well away from everybody else. I thought that, even if I screamed, although in the book there was always a second person to clap a hand over your mouth, nobody would hear me. Presumably there was a back way out, so no one would see me being carried away, gagged and insensible.

I knocked timidly and a deep voice said, 'Come in.'

I found myself facing an enormous man smoking an enormous cigar. He sat me down at a table and told me he didn't want shorthand, he wanted me to make three copies of an article written in a rather difficult handwriting. I was so nervous that at first I put all the carbons in the wrong way round, and when I discovered my mistake I went on with the page, in case he had eyes in the back of his head and saw me withdraw a half-typed sheet. I did not like to ask him when I was stumped as to what a word was meant to be – it would seem as though I criticised his writing, which was rude, or as if I myself were a fool, which would be worse. I made a guess when I was uncertain. The article was all about Jews; it would have given Hitler blood pressure. Mr Zimmerman considered that Jews in a community were the leaven leavening the whole lump. He wrote lyrically of their distinctive qualities – artistic, domestic, commercial. He seemed acquainted with the history of every prominent Jew since Moses. When I had finished he drew up a chair beside me and checked the article over. He said nothing when it became obvious that I had misread his writing, neither blaming me nor apologising for himself. I made the necessary alterations and heard him say I had done well. Outside I bought a bar of chocolate that I ate as I walked down Victoria Street, and then turned in to the office, for I had some important work of my own to deal with before the afternoon session began. To my surprise Miss G. had not gone out to lunch.

'Have you finished?' she demanded.

'Yes.'

'Did he want shorthand or typing?'

'Only typing.'

'I see. Have you had your lunch?'

I said yes before I could stop myself, and she looked at me rather suspiciously.

'I ask, because we charge by time. You must have been very quick.'

I thought of the page I had had to type twice over, and the time I had taken making the corrections.

'I don't think so.'

I felt it would be dreadful if she charged him too much. Miss G. tossed on her hat – all her hats were alike and any of them might have been washed up by a wreck – and went out. I dismissed all thoughts of Mr Zimmerman and uncovered the best of the learner's machines. I had written a poem on the original subject of 'June' with which I proposed to tempt various London magazines.

A day or two after that I was sent to Holborn to a dyeing firm. Here the work was more intricate. I had to copy long specifications of ingredients of British dyes. The typewriter was a very large one, and had signs I had never seen before. It was tabular work and a mistake meant ruining seven huge sheets. Nobody paid any attention to me, however, and presently I became absorbed. When I got back to Victoria Street Miss G. told me I should probably be wanted there the next morning, but later she got a telephone message to say they would not need any more assistance.

'You got on better than they expected,' she told me. 'They spoke well of you.'

The result of that was that the following week Miss G. stopped me as I was going out to lunch.

She said, 'I have heard of an opening for you. Miss M.' (who conducted a copying office at the other end of the street) 'requires a junior clerk. She is offering 25s. a week for three months, 27s. 6d. a week for three months and then 30s.'

I said at once, 'But I wish to start at 30s.'

Miss G. looked amazed as well as displeased. 'You have no experience,' she pointed out.

'Other people with no experience start at 30s.'

'And then you are extremely young.'

'I don't see what difference that makes.'

'I think you had better go and see Miss M. I have told her to expect you.'

'Would she be likely to start me at 30s., if I talked to her?'

'No. She is not prepared to do that for a junior.'

87

'Then it would be wasting her time and mine,' I pointed out reasonably, and departed.

Miss G. was gasping, but what else could I have said? This matter of a salary was a very sensitive one to me. Only a few days earlier I had said to a Grown-Up, being at that time in a state of extreme depression, 'Do you suppose I'll get as much as a pound a week?' to which the Grown-Up had replied in simple amazement, 'You? But how could you be worth a pound to any one?' How? I promised myself I wouldn't start at a pound, I would start at thirty shillings or die.

However, since I had treated Miss G.'s offer in what now appears a somewhat cavalier manner, I could hardly expect her to find me anything else. So I decided I had better go to an office and register my name for employment. I was handed an enormous form, with questions on both sides. The first few were easy. Name. Address. Age. Nationality. Where educated. After that I came to a dead stop.

Examinations taken. None, unless you counted the Junior Scholarship. The lady at the desk said you didn't. Degrees. None. University education. None. Qualifications. Shorthand 120. Typewriting 60. Book-keeping. I hesitated. I knew absolutely nothing about book-keeping. It had been included in the curriculum, but our teacher had been one of those unfortunate women who consider that the proper attitude towards inquiring youth is a sarcastic one. A question on some simple point brought a reply so devastating that you never asked another. Vague phrases floated through my head. Double entry. E. and O.E. Taking out the balance. I took up my pen and wrote: Simple. Languages. None. Other qualifications. None. Experience. None.

References. Another pause. You were not supposed to give the names of relatives. There was a Bishop in the family, my mother's brother, but he was on the other side of the world and 'Cannibal Islands' for an address would probably be treated as a bad joke. There was also a Brigadier-General, but he was at that time (I think) in Africa, and the same objection applied. Aunt Victoria had married a doctor who might 'speak for me', so I put his name down. Since it wasn't the same as mine, no one would know he was a relation. Now, who else? Father had a sister in a responsible position, but here the name difficulty applied. Purely social references I had none, not even a Vicar, who was always acceptable. Since we came to London eight years previously I could not remember seeing my parents put on evening dress or themselves give a party. My mother had a few women friends to tea now and again, but even these functions had become scarcer of recent years and now there was simply nobody. In desperation I put down the aunt whose name was the same as my own.

Salary required. Thirty shillings – to start, I added. Then I told the lady at the desk, I don't want a commercial job. I want something interesting.

My form was taken without comment and I went away. Nothing happened for some days, and then, in an evening paper two days old, we happened to see an advertisement from the Red Cross for a shorthand typist. I had promised myself never to answer advertisements, but the Red Cross, surely, was different. That couldn't have any connection with the W.S.T. My mother also liked the idea of my working for them in war-time. The advertisement said, Call at an address in Carlton House Terrace, and next morning I set out.

'I ought to have something better to wear than this old blue suit,' I suggested nervously, and indeed the skirt would have passed very well for one of those disfiguring mirrors you get in Fun Fairs.

'If you get this post you can buy something and pay for it out of your first two or three weeks' salary,' suggested my mother. 'But you had better be sure you will be able to pay for it first.'

That was sound common sense, so I took the clothes-brush for a rapid run round the hem of the skirt and set out. Although the Red Cross must be safe, my heart was beating like a trip-hammer as I went up the steps of the house in Carlton House Terrace where the Wounded and Missing Department of the Red Cross was housed. A plump woman, with yellow hair, told me to go down-stairs. The typing staff worked in the basement, many of them by electric light. Only the more fortunate sat by the windows, and needed no light before tea. Since the advertisement was already two days old I was afraid the vacancy might have been filled, but I was given a test and told to type it out, and then my name and address were taken, and I learned that I should hear later.

I went back to Miss G. and told her that I had applied for a job. She asked for the name of the woman I had seen, and dismayed me by saying, 'She was one of my pupils some years ago.' This seemed to me on the whole a pity, as in the circumstances I hardly expected Miss G. to find anything very good to say about me. However, at about four o'clock I was called to the telephone, and asked if I would work on a week's trial for 25s., my salary to be raised to 30s. if I were found satisfactory.

I said, 'I can count on the thirty shillings after the first week? Very well, then I will come tomorrow.'

I thought I might hear of nothing during that week, and this was approximately starting at the figure I had promised myself.

When I got home my mother was waiting for me, wearing her outdoor clothes.

'Don't make a story of it,' she said, as soon as I appeared. 'Just tell me whether you've got it or not.'

I said reluctantly that I had. I could have made a fine story out of that roomful of women, and my test, and the house generally.

She said, 'There isn't a minute to lose if you want to buy a new suit. We will go to John Barker's. It shuts at six.'

It was now half-past five. We went to Barker's by bus and I bought a fawn ready-made for 29s. 6d., obtained on credit, to be paid for out of my first two weeks' salary.

It didn't occur to my mother any more than it occurred to me that I should not be asked to stay on. She gave me a white cotton blouse with a narrow black pin-stripe, and we agreed that the imitation panama with its black ribbon would do for some time yet. The next morning I became a wage-earner.

I was astonished at the congratulations I received from my aunts, nearly all of whom wrote to me when they heard the news. They were particularly pleased that I was working for the Red Cross, instead of, as they had feared, for a firm that might be making money out of the war. I confessed to no one the enormous relief I felt – in my secret heart I had wondered whether any one would ever employ me.

I was attached to the Mediterranean Department, which dealt with Gallipoli casualties. In this department was Mr Howard Sturgis, the novelist, who didn't believe any woman ought to read his books. To my eyes he was quite an old man, with bushy white brows, white hair, and the general air of a rather elderly rabbit. He suffered intensely from the cold, I remember, always wearing a black overcoat and a white muffler to work in, and keeping his feet in a fur bag. He had an inexhaustible charm of manner and would make little jokes while he dictated. There was also in the same department a lady who astounded me by saying that until now she had never done her own hair; her maid had left her, either to get married or to do some form of war work, and she felt quite helpless.

It was a nice department and every one was kind, although I was embarrassed by the little lady for whom I chiefly worked, who talked, as the head mistress at school had done, about linking up our work with the sacrifices made by the men at the front, and pointed out to me that she and I were in a partnership and that if we didn't both play up we could not achieve the best results.

'I dictate the letters,' she said, 'and you type them, and if either of us does less than our best – well, you see, don't you?'

She was what the others called finicky, and didn't like signing a letter if a word had been halved at the end of a line.

Sometimes I helped in the French Department. Here I saw Mary Cholmondeley, whose novel *Red Pottage* I admired enormously. Her sister, Victoria, worked in the Mirror Room, and was one of the most striking women I have ever seen; tall and elegant, with a black velvet hat crowning wonderful white hair. Mary, on the other hand, was small and insignificant, a dumpy figure in dark blue. I felt it should have been Victoria who wrote novels and Mary who worked at the Red Cross. I still believed that authors should look more distinguished than other people.

It was in some ways rather a nightmare job with which to open one's career. The place was always full of women of every class, sitting in the hall, with slips of papers in their hands, asking for information about sons and husbands about whom, in six cases out of ten, nothing more was ever heard. Wounded and Missing was generally supposed to be pretty hopeless, Wounded and Missing, believed Killed, nearly always the same as Killed in Action or Died of Wounds. Now and again we had photographs of a man's grave, and these were always sent to relatives, who found them 'comforting'. At least it was a proof that they need hope no more, and that, of itself, brings a certain consolation.

I think it must have been that autumn that the Epoch-Making event occurred. I sold a poem and was paid for it – in cash. Christopher was home on leave from his training camp, and we had been to a theatre. On our return I saw an envelope addressed to myself leaning against the clock. I carried it upstairs to open in secret and found two enclosures. One was a letter which said:

Dear Madam,
We like the verses you have submitted to us, and herewith enclose payment at our usual rates.

The heading on the paper was the *Family Herald* and payment was a postal order for three-and-sixpence!

I was torn between pride at having made a professional sale (as apart from prizes in competitions) and shame at the smallness of the reward. I had read somewhere that Mrs Baillie Reynolds had begun her writing career in the *Family Herald*, so I thought it would be all right for me, too, and swallowed my pride at so humble a beginning.

Anyway, the *English Review*, which I was accustomed to bombard with long, Thompson-esque poems on social subjects, had never offered me even three-and-sixpence. All the same, I hadn't imagined I should ever be paid with anything less than a cheque.

The verses (there were three of them) were purely derivative and had no value whatsoever. On the whole, now, I think three-and-sixpence was good pay. They were this sort of thing:

> *A perfect rose,*
> *And then the fallen flower,*
> *But still, for just one hour,*
> *A perfect rose.*

Next day I wrote a business-like letter on my employer's typewriter, saying that I accepted their offer, and inquiring when they proposed to publish my contribution. The editor wrote back that he would send me a copy of the appropriate issue, but either he lied in his typewriter's teeth, or else he decided to cut his losses and not use the verses, for I never heard anything more about them.

The war years must have provided a magnificent harvest for the editors and publishers of a series of little paper-covered books called *Life's Harvest, The Upward Road*, and similar titles, which were collections of 'helpful' verse and prose; several of these were sent to me by relations and friends, and I copied a number of excerpts into the

Commonplace Book I began about this time. Never can there have been stranger bed-fellows than I collected there. John Oxenham's poems lay on every bookstall, and of course one of his volumes came to me through the post in due course.

> Is the burden past your bearing?
> God's in His Heaven!
> Helpless, friendless, no one caring?
> God's in His Heaven!
> Burdens shared are light to carry,
> Love shall come, though long he tarry,
> All's well, all's well,
> All's well!

Then a bit of Browning's 'Rabbi Ben Ezra' and then Ella Wheeler Wilcox, who would, I feel, have made him a wonderful wife.

> Hurry Up!
> No lingering by old doors of doubt,
> No loitering by the way,
> No waiting a Tomorrow car
> When you can board Today.
> Success is somewhere down the track,
> Before the chance is gone,
> Accelerate your laggard pace,
> Swing on, I say, swing on!
> Hurry up!

When I developed the Swinburne craze I copied one poem after another into the Book, but by 1920 I had had enough. The last entries were by Alfred Noyes, Rudyard Kipling, and myself.

I left the Red Cross in 1917 and in 1918 I was working in a Government office. At first I was in the Jam Department (it had a more lordly name on the records) and seeing Mr Blackwell of Crosse and Blackwell was like seeing some one out of a fairy-tale. The person I remember best from that time was a young lieutenant who had been invalided home, but was still in uniform. He was tall, dark, and morose, and had a perpetually haunted look. Even when he came down to the department to search through the records he didn't seem as though he saw any of us. I never heard him speak of his experiences, or indeed of anything but 'blood for cattle-cakes'.

I think some of the bolder spirits among the women tried to establish some sort of contact with him, but he did not seem to recognise our world. He seemed to me a personification of that war which, for all one's imagination, we really didn't know at all. When I think of that time it is his face that rises up instantly, although I never so much as knew his name. I wished I could wipe that look out of his eyes. He was probably about twenty-three and he looked as old as the world.

★

Let me here put one fact on record, dispel one illusion that seems to have been pretty generally held by those who never worked in offices. Office life is not romantic! It is not one giddy opportunity for matrimony. Men in offices are, for the most part, Deadly Bores. If they have a romantic side, they leave it at home. They are, as a rule, heavily wived and childrened; they suffer from indigestion and ask you to buy their pills in your lunch-hour. They write letters – some of them – to outfitters in remote places describing their peculiar requirements in the matter of pants and cholera belts; they seldom, if ever, think of their girl employees as human beings at all. What they would prefer, if they were procurable and didn't cost too much, would be a series of automatic machines, into which you put the week's salary and took out the letters at the other end. They would prefer these to young women, because you can kick a machine, if you happen to be put out about something, without being hauled into court for assault.

In more than eight years of office experience I came across two 'romances'. One was in the city where a timid, mousey little man, looking more than his alleged two-and-forty years, married a pretty girl twenty years his junior, and the other, after the war, when the groom was a high-stomached, purseproud widower, who persuaded (to my incredulous horror) an attractive Scotch girl of twenty-six to marry him. Apart from that, I have never seen a sign of romance in an office. Nor need girls entering that life imagine that their virtue will be threatened.

No employer cares a dump if you have virtue or not. If you have it you can keep it. He isn't out to buy it, anyway.

Films are written about lovely secretaries madly pursued by 'bosses', royalties are coined out of stories on the same theme – simply because there isn't a word of truth in it. And when you have seen most of the men you meet in offices your thoughts are more inclined to turn towards convents. The awful warnings (and delightful expectations) you receive always come from middle-aged relatives who have never been inside an office in their lives.

Chapter Six

Looking back, after twenty years, it astounds me to remember how often and how intensely I was happy during that time. None of the lighter side of war came our way; no parties, dances, whirlwind romances, adventures of any kind stand out from the recollection of that time. Life was a round of unremitting work – work at the office and work in the home. But presumably that very struggle for a living, the persistent anticipation of the future, the feeling that only youth knows that the present, so frequently unsatisfactory and drab, cannot be all – these things lent vitality to the days. The sense of personality remains very strong even in the heart of nationwide mourning. And even when hope seemed humbled, ambition remained. We, the war generation, who were young in 1914, and still young at the time of the Armistice, had grown up to accept war as our normal estate.

We tried to speculate sometimes as to what a peace-time world would be like, what on earth the pre-war papers had contained. It was not strange and dreadful to us, as it must have been to our parents, to see long lines of young men in khaki marching through London: we did not miss the ease, the security, the rich leisureliness of life that people of our class had enjoyed before the war, because we had never experienced it. You can live in a past that was once yours, but you can't live in a past you never knew.

Certainly there was little enough, at home or abroad, to make one gay, and yet, riding up to work on a No. 33 bus, noting that the chestnut-trees in the park had advanced a stage since the previous morning, had turned back their rosy sheaths and put out green flames of leaves, I would be consumed with delight.

'Whatever life does to me, whatever I may have to endure, this can never be taken from me,' I exulted to myself, 'this I shall always remember.' Poverty, old age, blindness even (blindness was one of my secret terrors) could not rob me of it.

Ethel Mannin in her book, *Confessions and Impressions*, speaks of living by a secret sun in her own breast. I have heard the phrase condemned as journalese, but the author was writing of what she knew. That groundless, irrational sense of joy that has no definite foundation and that could not be explained – even now it assails me sometimes, when I have left youth behind me, and there is a shadow of a yet worse war ahead.

Even after Christopher went to France in 1917 and the

tension instantly tightened I could not escape that sense of ecstasy at just being alive.

He was in the tank action of November of that year, when it was reported that a hundred tanks were lost; for several days we had no news; each night, as I put my key into the lock, I found myself thinking, 'Perhaps the telegram came today.' But after more than a week of waiting we got a field postcard and knew that he was safe.

But from then on telegrams assumed for us the aspect they had had for millions of other people since the outbreak of war. One evening, coming back to a dark and empty house, for my mother and Joan were away and I was keeping house for Father, I found a telegram in the box. The boys put them there if they could get no reply. I stood for about three minutes in the dark, before I dared open the envelope. I tried to remember all those other women who had had similar wires and had found the courage to endure them. When at last I opened the envelope, the message said: 'Am coming up to town for two nights. Hope you can put me up.' And when I looked at the address I saw that it was not intended for me at all, but for my next-door neighbour.

I think I was most keenly aware of the war during the spring of 1918, when all the news seemed bad, and the papers were swamped with the lists of the casualties. It was rumoured everywhere that Paris would fall; people swore they could hear the rumble of the long-range guns. Then, perhaps for the first time, my imagination awoke, and I was tormented with the thought of the thousands of houses where young feet would never come again and young voices ring. Not enough now to read the poems of Katharine Tynan – 'The Young Knights of Paradise' – and the one beginning:

> *Lest Heaven be filled with greybeards hoary,*
> *God, who made boys for His delight,*
> *Stoops in a day of grief and glory*
> *And calls them home, home through the night …*

Even Rupert Brooke's famous sonnets lost much of their power to invest war in a robe of nobility. Besides, we were learning a little – not much, but a little – of what modern warfare could be. Years afterwards, when I read the war novels, I thought that if we had known the truth at the time, we could not have preserved our sanity. It cost the young men their youth, even if they weren't killed, even if, like Christopher, they were not even wounded. The first time he came home on leave he was nineteen, and he looked thirty. Youth seemed wiped clean out of his face.

That year – 1918 – I changed my job again, becoming secretary to Mr (now Sir Sylvanus) Vivian, liaison-officer between the newly created National Health Ministry and the British Medical Association. It was while I was here that I met a woman who said to me, 'You can make the most trivial letter look as though it meant something. It's a pity you don't do anything with your brains.'

I was startled. 'I don't know what you mean.'

'You waste them so. You trifle with life.'

'What do you think I ought to do?' I asked. I was still a bit indignant.

'Why don't you study economics? They are contemporary history. It ought to matter to you – the conditions under which your fellows live. How are things ever to become better if people like you don't care?'

That was Angel Lawrence at the beginning of 1919. She did not offer to lend me any books on economics, but she gave me E. M. Forster's *Celestial Omnibus*, a book I found so enthralling that I began to think there might be something in her other idea, too.

The Armistice was by that time two months old, and we were all beginning to think about the future. Just as I had not been prepared for the war, so I was not prepared for the Armistice. The war had gone on for so long I was dazed to think that it might be over. When the maroons sounded at eleven o'clock I was swept away with the general wave of insane rejoicing. I dashed down into the street and bought a flag – it was bright blue with a sort of gold pineapple on it, and I vaguely supposed it represented one of our lesser-known allies. A mass of us waved this madly from our third-floor window, and crowds of people in the Strand yelled madly back.

We were still shouting like dervishes when Mr Vivian came in and attracted my attention. He explained that this was probably going to be the busiest day of our lives.

The influenza scourge was ravishing the country, and we had to get as many doctors as possible back from France in record time. I sat down and typed the necessary slips in triplicate. All round me the noise went on, until the rest of the office swept out to a lunch-hour much earlier than its usual time. Miss Lawrence commandeered me presently to do some letters for her. Conditions in the country were unspeakable; corpses lay for days unburied because there was no doctor to sign the necessary certificates; the association was bombarded with appeals. Locums, no matter how weak their qualifications, were worth their weight in gold. It was urgently represented that now our need was greater than that of the Army.

It was late when I went out to lunch, but so far as getting any food was concerned I might as well have stayed in the office. No one was attempting to execute orders. In Lyons' Corner House waitresses danced with officers in uniform. I danced myself in a crazy ring, between a little woman, whose *embonpoint* threatened to burst her tight silk blouse, and a tall captain of infantry. In the streets the buses were packed with people who didn't know their destinations and didn't care. You had the odd spectacle of buses with 'II' on the front rumbling up Regent Street. The driver of a bus I passed, a bus with people seated all up the steps, and a golden-haired girl riding on the bonnet, said firmly, 'This bloody bus is going to 'Yde Park Corner and it's bloody well going to stay there.' I think it was labelled Hackney Wick. When the driver said that all the passengers cheered, and some one started 'For he's a jolly good fellow'.

A taxi full of young officers, several inside and several more on the roof, joined in, and some of them shouted to me to come aboard. But I shook my head. The Armistice might be sheer relief to these people, but I had national work to do. I didn't feel pleased or proud about this, only sorry I couldn't stop to join in the general lunacy. The world does not contain as many nations as there were flags flourished in the streets that day; very few of them had any national significance.

The office was more than half empty. The Government offices, except for essential services, were closing down until the morning. They knew, I suppose, they would get no sane work out of their staffs that afternoon. Soon rain began to fall and the crowds in the streets thinned. Mr Vivian said we had to get over to the Windsor Hotel for a conference that had been hastily convened to get back men from France. I was to act as shorthand writer. All the services were represented; there was an Admiral, with a monocle on a thin black cord, a General with red tabs, Sir James Galloway in the Chair, Mr Aubrey Vere Symonds, looking as immaculate as his name, hosts of others whose names I either never knew or have forgotten. The conference lasted until about five, and then I was able to go home.

The next few days we were rushing doctors over from France, and trying to cope with the hundreds of letters that poured in from all over the country, begging for medical assistance. Doctors themselves contracted the disease and died, so to speak, on their feet. One of them, rushing back from his rounds, found his young daughter of seventeen at her last gasp; he signed a certificate, wrote to the authorities pleading for assistance, and went out again. Men who had fought against going to France were now reluctant to return; many who did wanted to go back immediately to their own practices. We drafted men, as we could, where they were most desperately needed; we worked full strength with card indices and telephone calls day after day until the tremendous pressure slackened. Then I reminded myself that the war was over and I must look for another job.

One queer effect the peace had upon me. Although I was only nineteen, not much older than my mother had been at her coming-out ball, all at once I ceased to think of myself as young. Youth and the war had been synonymous terms. Now the war was over and youth had vanished with it.

I could have stayed with Mr Vivian, but in that case I should have to come on the strength as an ordinary clerk at a wage of, I think, 35s. a week. At that time I was earning 54s., and was ambitious. I went to a new Employment Bureau and found the waiting-room packed with women of all shapes and sizes, waiting to be interviewed. One of them, aged about fifty, was talking in a loud voice about the desirability of a lethal chamber for unwanted workers.

'Take my case,' she invited us. 'I'm a chartered account-
ant. My father spent a great deal of money getting me
trained, and then I travelled for two years to perfect my
languages. I've never been able to save, but no one will
employ me. What am I to do?'

I thought if she bought herself a pair of corsets it
would be a step in the right direction.

I waited there while one woman after another disappeared into the room across the passage; all the time
other women were pouring in. I wondered how much
chance I should have of any vacancies that might be
going. At last it was my turn. The lady in charge asked
me what sort of work I wanted, and I said, a secretaryship. She asked me what I had done, and I told her. Then
she asked me how old I was. I had just had my twentieth
birthday.

'Ah well,' she said patronisingly, 'that's rather young for
a responsible post. But I'm sure we shall be able to find
you something quite interesting.'

I went away, promising myself that I would apply for
nothing she sent me. Two days later she let me know
(per a carbon-typed slip) that a branch of Macfisheries
wanted a shorthand-writer. I put the damned insult in
the basket. She sent me two or three more of the same
kind, and they all met with a similar fate. Then she sent
me news of a good post. And after that another. I realised
what had happened. She had heard from Mr Vivian –
subsequently I saw his reply and understood her swift
change of front – and had decided that I was worthy of

consideration. But I stuck to my decision, and answered none of her offers. Meanwhile I had returned to my original employment bureau, and was urged to take a job in an engineer's office. Good pay and only three other women in the room.

'With a woman in charge, I suppose?' I said.

'No one is really in charge,' said Miss M. evasively. 'You all work together.'

'I understand. Actually I wanted a secretaryship.'

She told me they were very hard to get, particularly if you were young. I said, I am twenty, you know, and decided I'd wait. But the days went by, and nothing better offered, and I began to reconsider the job. I went to see her again, in case something else had turned up, but this was still the best post she could offer me. I might have been secretary to a Church dignitary for a regular two pounds a week, or lived in Lowndes Square, done all the secretarial work, looked after the housekeeping and been responsible for a number of dogs and cagebirds for forty pounds a year, but I said I wasn't a slave and what had we won the war for, anyway?

I had almost decided to yield and take the engineer's job (I never doubted that they would have me) when I happened to go into Christ Church, the Church on the Green, where someone – I think it was Father Bull of the Mirfield Fathers – preached a sermon that sent me out declaring that at all costs I would stick to my guns. I wrote definitely that I was not interested in the engineer's office, and settled down to wait.

I did not have to wait long. The following afternoon I received a telephone call from a man whose office I had visited about ten days earlier, but who had apparently not been impressed by my written application. He asked whether I could come to interview him at Temple Chambers at once. I obtained the requisite permission, but was discomfited to find that all the flats on the fourth floor had private tenants. Men were dashing in and out, men of all kinds. My old companions, the White Slave Traders, reared their heads. I remembered that I had been told the Agency had no knowledge of this man and if I asked for an interview with him I did it at my own risk. The papers had warnings of adventurers of all nations in our midst; the demobilised men had gratuities and, often enough, little sense of money; there was a harvest to be got there if you knew how to set to work. And men about whom nobody knew anything were always Risky.

I pulled myself together at last and rang the bell; as usual, this office was at the end of a corridor and a little away from all the rest. The door was opened at once by a young man with the longest eyelashes I have ever seen. He said affably, 'Oh, do come in. I'm sorry my man has just gone out.'

The room into which he led me was clearly no office; it was far too comfortably furnished; through an open door across the passage I saw a combined bathroom–lavatory; I sat down squarely in a deep chair and thought, 'The next quarter of an hour may determine my whole life.' It had poured earlier in the day and my heavy purple frieze coat was dark with rain; my sturdy black shoes were mud-encrusted; I still wore sensible black stockings of lisle thread; even my hat failed miserably to betray the fact that it had cost 27s. 6d., an unheard-of price for me; I had spent a whole week's housekeeping on it. It was a fawn-coloured velour, turned up at the back; this brim collected water like a leaking boat; when I twitched it carelessly off on my return from lunch a heavy stream of icy rain ran down my back, and my clothes were still wet from it.

I drew some consolation from my companion's omission to close the door, though I remembered that the outer door shut with a Yale lock. He stood opposite me, leaning negligently against the fireplace, and told me a good deal of his own history, his father's views as well as his own on social economics; he asked me when I would be free and what I was doing now. After this, he said it was very nice of me to call and he would let me know. It struck me as odd that he had not mentioned salary. Obviously someone had to speak of it, so I did; but a bit timidly, because I still believed that only two kinds of people ever talked openly about money – clergymen in pulpits and cads everywhere.

He said, airily, 'Oh yes, of course. How much do you want?'

I named the very highest sum I had dared to suggest to any agency, and he said, 'Yes, I'm sure that would be all right. Well, you'll be hearing from me.'

On the way down in the lift I couldn't make up my

mind whether he was an honest man, without business experience, or the other thing, who had decided I wasn't worth the risk. A day or two later I got my letter, saying that, subject to references being satisfactory, I was employed at the figure I had named. I still had another week with Mr Vivian. Other girls in that office were getting settled and going off to new jobs; practically every one had definite plans. I began to get anxious. Unemployment was one of the luxuries I couldn't afford. The last day came and still I had heard nothing. At half-past twelve I received a telephone call.

'Captain V—— speaking. Could you start this afternoon at two-thirty?'

I hunted up the head of the department. 'Could I have this afternoon off, do you think? Mr Vivian won't be coming back, and I've cleared up everything.'

The head thought I could. 'Don't forget to go over to the Windsor and collect your pay,' he reminded me. He needn't have troubled. When he heard why I wanted the afternoon, his attitude changed.

'I don't think you ought to do that,' he said. 'I thought you wanted to go to a show.'

Shows on a week-day afternoon, I thought, in a world where you've got to get your living! That day I pulled off the first smart bit of business I had ever achieved. I only worked half a day for each party, and both paid me for a full day's work.

My new employer was waiting for me. He took me into an inner room and volunteered the information that this was Sir Edward Ward's private flat, and that he had lent it until suitable offices could be obtained.

It occurred to me for the first time that I had no idea what this business was about. My first few letters, however, shed a little light. At that time the Sankey Commission was sitting to decide the tremendous question of the nationalisation of the mines. During the war these had been taken over by the Government, and the debate was now whether they should be handed back to their original owners or whether certain compensation should be paid, and the coal supplies of the country belong to the nation. There was a very strong party holding this last view. They published innumerable leaflets to show that the profits made by private enterprise were quite disproportionate to the rewards the men themselves earned; coal, they argued, was a basic industry; it was, indeed, the foundation of almost every other trade, and they resented a bunch of private individuals having such colossal control over the affairs of the nation. They declared that pre-war profits were so enormous that the coal owners dared not allow them to be made public.

It was a political as well as an economic battle, in which public opinion was bound to play a large part. The Coal Association represented the owners and private enterprise generally. It was got together very quickly as a defensive measure. Soon it flooded the country with propaganda. Neither side seemed to be particularly scrupulous in their methods; the Miners' Federation said that the owners were out for tremendous profits for themselves and for the shareholders at the expense of the safety of the men; the owners retorted that anything the Government touched it ruined. Of course, there were disinterested men on both sides, but between them they issued enough leaflets to have papered the whole of Whitehall. The Coal Association, as this new arm was called, consisted of a director, who was also a publicity expert, his secretary, Captain V—— and myself – that is, we were the personnel. The Association itself numbered all manner of great names, and in a very short time it swelled into a large organisation with a Press Department, a Statistical Department, and a big typing staff.

That first afternoon I wrote letters until about five o'clock, when Captain V—— came in and said, 'You're not in a hurry, I hope? We've got to go to a conference.'

Outside, by the kerb, a magnificent car was waiting. My spirit was sufficiently broken by three years of wage-earning to suggest my standing aside while the mighty, all men, stepped into the vehicle, but they waved me into the best seat, and we drove off to a flat in St James's. Here we walked down a long rose-red corridor into a room full of deep divans in sapphire velvet, cushions like snow mountains, and paintings on the walls of gods and messengers falling, like Lucifer, from a cloudy Heaven, blowing trumpets as they came. Blokes drinking beer head downwards was a less poetic description of them.

Tea was spread on the table, and with tea, marmalade sandwiches. I sipped tea, nibbled a sandwich, my eyes popping out of my head. More men kept coming in, sitting down, exchanging conversation. Things were pretty serious; the Public Must Be Warned. Presently there entered the man for whom the rest had been waiting, a big dour man of the Arnold Bennett Five Towns period, I thought, with a great black moustache with long drooping ends, and a manner like a ton weight.

'They've made appreciable progress at the Commission today,' he began, and then his eye fell on me. 'Who is the lady?' he demanded.

Sir Alan (then Mr) Hutchings leaned forward. 'The lady, Mr T., is one of us.'

Mr T. nodded. He was a fascinating creature; he looked as though he had been plucked straight out of Madame Tussauds.

'Don't mind my asking,' he rumbled.

Oh no, I assured him, I didn't mind – nodding my head in its bright blue straw helmet, with a classy spray of pink cotton convolvulus in the front.

The conference began; I was there as shorthand-writer, to get down a verbatim report. Many of the expressions they tossed across the tea-table meant nothing to me then; royalties, mineral royalties, shareholders, dividends, the cost of maintenance, safety-men, pumps, safety-lamps that the owners had insisted on being used in spite of the apathy of the workers. My pencil flew; I wondered a bit dubiously what I should make of some of those outlines later on. Still, I was accustomed to this sort of thing. I had acted in a similar capacity at the Ministry of Food and later at the Ministry of National Service. About seven o'clock the conference broke up, to assemble again at the same time tomorrow. My head was swimming.

Captain V—— said briskly, 'Not tired, I hope,' and we whizzed back in a taxi to Temple Chambers. Here I transcribed my minutes and sent a copy to all the principals who had attended the meeting. I made a grand story of the afternoon when I got home.

The next night it pelted and taxis were hard to come by. Captain V—— was in a perverse mood.

'Hope there won't be much more of this chin-wagging,' he said. 'Don't see much use in all this talk myself. I'm an Army man. Deeds, not words, that's our motto.'

That second night I sat next to a gentleman who looked a cross between Edward VII and Mr Jorrocks. This person said kindly, 'Are you responsible for these?' and tapped the minutes of yesterday's meeting.

'Yes,' said I.

'Congratulate you,' said the personage.

I have always blushed much too easily. I felt like a stupid schoolgirl. To offset that treacherous change of colour (with pleasure at the compliment) I laughed lightly.

'Oh, minutes are my strong suit,' I told him.

Later on I asked Captain V—— who the personage was.

'That old boy? That was Sir Edward Ward. Big bug in the police.'

I decided that simple affirmatives and negatives were probably safest in that company.

Alas, there were no more meetings. Or at least, we attended none. But some of the gentlemen, notably a tall thin one called Tommy, came over to Temple Chambers and warbled war-hits while he dictated.

'Katie, beautiful K-Katie,' he sang. 'Here, tell these blighters we're not the relieving officers, will you? You know – the way Whitehall does. Have you seen the new George Robey show? Oh, but you should.'

And, hands in pockets, he whistled his way out again.

Chapter Seven

I was sorting the contents of the staff file, that was marked Private, and made the disconcerting discovery that the director's typist was being paid more than I was. Not his secretary, who was a rather brilliant woman with a University degree, but his typist. I felt there was something wrong about that. Not that I was mercenary, of course, but I was Yorkshire, with a dash of Scotch, and if money was being given away it seemed a sin to let it waste. The obvious person to approach was Captain V——. As he had agreed to my figure without demur I felt this must be delicately done.

'When you want something out of a man, look your best,' a well-wisher advised me. The powder-blue suit and the bright blue hat were my best, but I laid out one-and-ninepence on a length of stiff powder-blue tulle. My mother always wore tulle – she was mainly dressed in etceteras, tulle and fringe and flowers and feathers and floating hand-painted scarves – and I knew that tulle, if uncomfortably rigid and apt to be sticky when damp, was the *dernier cri* in elegance.

I decided to wait until the end of the day to open the subject. Then, if my request were refused, I could put on my hat and go home, but to work all day with this embarrassing question of money between us would probably have a bad effect on my work. Walking down the Strand at lunch-time I met an erstwhile colleague.

'You're looking like a duchess,' said she. 'What are you getting now? Five pounds a week?'

'Well, not yet.'

But no reason, so far as I could see, why eventually I shouldn't. The remark comforted me. A duchess! That was the effect I wanted to produce. Even so it was difficult. It never became easy to talk casually about money. Still, on this occasion, it had to be done.

'Oh, by the way, Captain V——' a light and careless opening, I thought, 'when I was sorting your staff file I couldn't help seeing that Miss R. gets ten shillings a week more than I do.'

'I suppose the director made the arrangement,' said V——, a bit on the defensive.

'I suppose so.'

'You're getting what you asked, aren't you?'

'Oh, I am. It's just that I thought it might seem a bit queer, the director's typist getting more than the secretary's secretary.'

That was the right move. There was a secret jealousy between the two offices.

'I'll look into it,' he promised at once.

Twenty-four hours later he went down with influenza. Well, I supposed, that was the fortunes of war. Influenza does amazing things to people, makes them forgetful and queer and never, never could I summon courage to raise the point again. But at the week's end the book-keeper said, 'By the way, I congratulate you. I've been told to give you a rise in screw.'

'Oh, really.' I tried to sound disinterested. Screw, indeed!

'Another quid a week as from today.'

That was doing the handsome thing. Four pounds a week at twenty with no languages, no book-keeping, no special qualifications of any kind, was something of an achievement. This was clearly the office I had been looking for.

Even after the conferences stopped the work continued to be amusing. The staff swelled by leaps and bounds and all the new men wanted secretaries. Secretaries just then were hard to come by, though a year later you could pick them like blackberries.

'Don't know any one, I suppose, who wants a job?' They would come along to my room and ask me that.

Oh, it was fun, after filling in forms and being told you were too young to be a secretary but no doubt they would fit you up with something Quaite Interesting, to ring up those very employment bureaux, give your name, and say, 'I want some additional staff,' with a list of necessary qualifications and stated hours when they could be interviewed. It was enlightening, too, to hear some of these business men doing the interviewing, for when anyone promising arrived, the prospective employer was called in to talk to her. There was a man there who looked like Mr Micawber, the same tall stiff figure, the same odd-shaped face with the plume of hair on top. He was one of the men who needed a secretary. One afternoon a young married woman who seemed suitable arrived. I went to find this man.

'I say,' remarked Mr L. anxiously, as he fell into step, 'd'you think she's really any good? Well, I suppose you do, or you wouldn't have called me. What does she look like? Not one of these women with a bosom you could rest a tea-tray on? That's good. I don't care for the anchovy fork type myself, but there are limits.'

The interview took this form.

Mr L. 'I say, can you take down letters in shorthand?'

N. or M. 'Oh, yes.'

Mr L. 'Well, I expect you can, but can you read them back?'

N. or M. 'I think so.'

Mr L. 'Actually, it's rather important that you should, because the girl we've got now can take 'em down like winking, but she can't read 'em back, not as we dictated them, and we rather like to be able to recognise our letters, just recognise 'em, you know. If we can't, old B,' (Mr L.'s room-mate) 'just tears out his hair, and between ourselves, the old boy can't afford to lose any more hair.'

He approved of this applicant, but she was now doubtful. 'Do you think he's really all right?'

'Oh yes,' I assured her, 'that's just his way.'

But it wasn't all fun. The young, haughty applicants, who had had fat easy jobs during the war, were easy to dispose of, but when the middle-aged tide began to flow in, women struggling desperately to stay in employment at all costs, only too painfully willing to accept any conditions – no, it wasn't funny then.

For, in place of the disillusion of war, we now had the disillusion of peace. After that first year, when there was work to be had for the asking, the labour market was appallingly overcrowded. Part of this state of affairs was due to the fact that its scope was immeasurably wider. The army of women, who had flooded into offices between 1914–18, could not be shooed back to their homes, like a flock of hens. Demobilised soldiers declared bitterly that, not satisfied with allowing men to risk their lives for them in war, they were now thrusting them towards starvation in peace. But the women retorted, in thousands of cases with justice, that the men who would have been their natural breadwinners lay in France and Gallipoli or in the sea.

But there was more to it than that. The war had brought women all those privileges that the Suffragettes had fought for so fiercely. It was true that the vote, when it came, was at first granted only to women of thirty or over, in order to equalise the numbers of voters of both sexes, but anger was growing among the younger women. If I'm old enough to pay taxes on the income I earn, I'm old enough to have some say in the way that money's spent. That was the burden of their cry. I said it myself before ever Mr Baldwin agreed to give votes, irrespective of sex, on the attainment of the majority.

An extra burden on the labour market was the number of men who, in another generation, had belonged to the rank of the voluntarily unemployed, men with private means, with estates, with no necessity to work for a living. The chaotic state of affairs after the war swept most of them into the market, too. Taxes were enormous, one big estate after another was sold for building purposes. For, in addition to no work, there were no homes for thousands of returned men. The unscrupulous reaped a rich harvest; a slip of linoleum and a broken-backed chair turned an attic into a furnished room, for which a totally disproportionate rent could be asked. Another advantage about letting your rooms furnished was that you could eject your tenants at a week's notice. In unfurnished rooms, you had to allow them to remain until they could find alternative accommodation. Key-money among the poor, and the system of premiums among the richer – i.e. the middle and upper classes – became the order of the day. Enormous sums would be asked for fittings, and even after premiums became illegal, owners would leave some curtain poles and a strip of carpet in their rooms and insist that 'fittings' should be bought.

One man, newly free from the army, told me in 1920

that he had asked a wage of 50s. a week, and had been laughed at.

'I can get all the men I want for thirty bob a week,' he had been told.

Distress was widespread, not only among those getting dangerously near forty – Too Old at Forty was beginning to be chanted everywhere – but among those who were much older. During the war, when labour was at a premium, they had found employment with little trouble; and now that the war was over and Government offices dismissing their staffs *en bloc*, they discovered that annuities or dividends that had been sufficient in 1913 were totally ludicrous now. No, it was speedily obvious that Peace and Paradise were by no means synonymous terms.

One's individual viewpoint had shifted, too. Once it had been enough to have a job oneself, be independent, but now one began to develop a sense of corporate responsibility. Even faith in oneself was not enough. One sick cell in the body can generate disease to all the living cells, and there were sick cells on every hand. For some time conscience had been salved by setting aside a tenth of one's earnings, kept in a Vinolia soapbox and carefully labelled, so that in the event of accident the few shillings thus saved should reach their appointed destination, but retaining nine-tenths for oneself had begun to seem niggardly and cheap. It wasn't by reading the books on economics that Angel Lawrence had suggested, but seeing the social machine in action that one's peace of mind became so grievously disturbed.

The family is a unit, said the social workers; but now the family itself seemed no more than a unit in a huge family, many of whose members were starving. Reading only made matters worse; you could be horrified by a book like Frank Hodges' history of coal-mining at the beginning of the century, when women, clad only in their shifts, crawled on all fours through the pits, harnessed to little carts; but although legislation had put a stop to that, nothing, it seemed, could be done for this growing army of Unemployed.

You could not escape them, in the offices. First of all, there were the old men, the jolly old buffers of pre-war days, in their skirted coats of a rather bright blue, their whitey-yellow moustaches, their hats with curly brims, their suggestion of a dashing manner concealing their very real dread of the future. Whenever you wanted odd staff for filling in cards or addressing envelopes, they rolled up. Life in the old dog yet, they said, don't want to go on the shelf before me time, you're dead for the rest of your days, they chuckled. Two pounds ten – well, they'd take it, they'd take it. Times weren't what they had been. Some of them had tiny pensions, some pitiful savings practically exhausted.

They weren't any good. With the best will in the world you had to acknowledge that. They hadn't been bred to ledger or desk. One was an old ex-army officer who had commuted his pension; others hinted at country house youths, gaieties that existed only in books for the generation that grew up during the war. They meant well, but they could not find the necessary application. They became restless, talked too much, didn't like working with women, wouldn't in any circumstances work under women. They couldn't be kept on the strength, and one after another they went, jaunty to the last. One didn't hear of them again, but oh Heaven, how one wondered what their next step would be. They were the relics of a dead world. You only found them nowadays on the music-halls, the mashers of the 'nineties who had lived too long. Some of them had lost the sons, on whom they had counted, in the war; they were flotsam and jetsam in a world that had no room for them.

Worse still was the position of the men back from the Front, the educated classes who had positions to keep up, men whose youth had been spent in France, and who now wanted an opportunity to settle down to a civilian life, marry, beget children. We saw those, too.

It had been decided to employ a chartered account-ant as book-keeper, and one of the Officers' Associations had been approached. Applicants for the job poured in, in British warms and naval overcoats tactfully dyed, but betraying their origin in every line. These were, for the most part, quiet enough. They sat in a corner until it was their turn to be interviewed. They would answer any question, accept practically any salary. There were so many of them that Captain V—— suggested presently that his secretary might 'give them the once-over', get them to note down on a slip of paper their qualifications and personal details.

'So that I can wash out the duds,' he explained.

'Oh, no.' I was horrified.

'What do you mean?'

'They wouldn't like it.'

'They? You mean, you wouldn't like it.'

'No. I mean them.'

'What are you talking about?'

'I'm a girl and much younger. They won't want to tell me things. Men don't.'

But Captain V—— had no patience with that sort of thing. I mean to say, a man looking for a job is a man looking for a job, you know, and if they're accustomed to discipline, they're not likely to behave like debutantes at their first party. So after that, as the men came in, I handed them slips of paper and asked them to put down a few essential details.

They all asked the same question. 'Is the job filled yet?'

'Not yet.'

A kind of flicker of hope would give vitality to their carefully guarded expressions. None of them made any fuss; perhaps they were used to being asked this sort of thing by girl secretaries. When their turn came they went quickly into the inner room, and there was never anything in those graven faces as they came out to show how the interview had gone off.

'Good morning,' they said politely from the door, and I would say 'Good morning' without meeting their eyes.

'Devil of a lot of them,' commented Captain V——. 'Poor chaps!'

The last to come was a man older than most, with close-cropped sandy hair and sandy lashes, and a face like a bulldog. Most of them had been too quiet; this one could not sit still.

'Oh yes, rather, of course,' he said, when I told him about the slip. 'Jolly good idea.'

I bent over the typewriter; I could see him watching me, and hesitating. Oh God, let me off just this time. Don't let him ask ... But, of course, he did.

'I suppose – the job isn't filled yet, is it?'

'Not yet.'

'Well, that's something.' He passed the slip back. 'Will that be all right? Is there anything I've left out?'

I looked at what he had written. An ex-captain in the tanks. (Christopher had been in the tanks. Christopher was lucky. He was out in Malaya planting rubber, and so far the slump had not cost him his job.) Two children. Thirty-seven years old. Something occurred to me, I forget what. I suggested it, and he took the paper back with a sickening eagerness.

'Oh, rather, silly of me.'

Now there was nothing to do but wait. He looked at me hopefully. I made my fingers fly upon the keys and they rose up and jammed. My shorthand outlines made no sense; I dared not stop typing for fear he would speak again. It was that humble look I couldn't bear. I went on typing gibberish. I could copy the letter after he had gone. I could feel my heart beating like a drum, the sweat breaking out on my forehead. Why on earth didn't the last applicant come out? If Captain V—— kept him so long it looked as though he meant to engage him. Oh, be quick, I muttered, for in a minute surely this man would speak again. Of course he did.

'I say – d'you think there's a chance of my getting the job?'

What could I say? 'Captain V—— hasn't chosen any one yet.'

'I suppose there have been crowds?'

'A fair number.'

'I expected so. Haven't had a job since the war, not in my own line, that is. Oh well, there's a good time coming.'

He couldn't keep quiet. It was no use blaming him. He was simply racked with anxiety. I thought no one could blame him if he suddenly got up and raged at me, at the young girl (actually I was twenty-two, but some people still seemed to think that young), who had never heard a shell fired or seen a friend blown to bits, who didn't have nightmares or hear dead men screaming in the dark, who stayed at home safe and sound during the war because this man and thousands like him thought it was his job to protect me and my kind. It didn't make sense, whichever way you looked at it. It was absurd to suppose that I could be more valuable than he, with two children to support and good qualifications and pre-war experience. Yet there I was, drawing my safe four pound ten a week, wearing a frock that was new that morning and had cost me four guineas, the most expensive frock I had ever had, pretending to transcribe a letter and knowing that on Friday my money would be waiting for me, and the Friday after that, and the one after that and so on, God help us all, till Kingdom Come. Quite possibly, though, he wasn't thinking any of these things. Probably it was only my fevered imagination, my own sense of shame at being so healthy, so safe, in such a pretty dress. I tried to believe that.

The inner door opened and the last applicant came out. Same graven smile, same polite nod as he took up his hat. The ginger-headed man began to rise, but Captain V—— was beckoning to me secretly. I slipped into his room.

'Who's that chap? I can't see any more tonight.'

'Can't you just see this one? He's been here such ages and he won't keep you more than a minute.'

'If he's any good, he will. Let's see his slip. My dear girl, that's no good. Thirty-seven. Much too old.'

'It only means he's had more experience.' How could I go back and see the last vestige of hope die out of that pale, twitching face?

'No *bon*. Four hundred a year isn't going to keep a man and his wife and two kids. I hardly know how to get along on twice that, and I've only got Junior. No, if I take any one it'll be that naval chap who came first. Twenty-eight. A nice fellow. Get rid of this lad. You know how to do it. Say I've got to keep an appointment.'

The red-headed man knew it was all U.P. as soon as I opened the door.

'It's all fixed?' he suggested, as I hesitated on the threshold.

'I'm awfully sorry. Captain V—— has to go out. He's late as it is.'

'I understand ... Oh well.' He took up his hat. One more smile that tells you nothing, one more good night, one more second and he'll have gone. But he hadn't. At the door he turned and came back to my table. He held out his hand.

'I say – you've been awfully decent. Don't – don't mind so much.'

I hadn't known before how rotten it could be to be safe when other people were in danger, and there was nothing you could do.

To some of us who never seemed to come into direct touch with the war, to whom it was a matter of getting jobs and working hard and keeping a roof over our heads, and who still foresaw hope in the future, it was the peace rather than the war that was the Great Illusion. The Church had taught, between 1914 and 1918, that it was possible to unite the sacrifices of men in a righteous cause with the sacrifice of Christ on Calvary for the salvation of the world, but now that the war was over and it was obvious that the world had not been won for righteousness, that distress and hunger and greed and despair were everywhere abroad, starvation in Austria, poverty in Germany, unemployment in our own country, everywhere men's hearts failing them for fear, even that consolation was lost.

Conceivably that earlier suffering might have some spiritual value, but no cause could be strengthened by this senseless post-war misery. Of all the war books I have read, nothing moved me more than the last page of Willa Cather's *One of Us*. The deliberate simplicity, the absence of passion in her description of the despair of the post-war world would chill the warmest blood.

Yet human nature was appallingly recuperative. Walking through the park a few days later, after a night of snow, stimulated by the keen tang in the air and the frosty sun in the sky, the old familiar sense of joy came flooding back. No concentration on the griefs of other men could stem it. Yet I felt it was wrong to be so happy. Life, I thought, was too easy. One had all the essential things – a roof (not a particularly good roof, for the landlord had done nothing for seven years, except drop the rent ten pounds on condition that no repairs were asked for, with the result that in wet weather one shifted one's bed and put a basin on the floor where the roof leaked); one had food and clothes and a job, and one still believed incurably in one's future. In those years I never said, *if* I succeed, I said, *when* I succeed. That was the real thing that separated one from men like the sandy-haired man. I had faith and hope and he hadn't got either any more. I had known that the instant he came in. He didn't really expect to get the job, he didn't expect to get anything any more.

You could, if your conscience hurt you too much, go without lunch and put the money in the poor box, you could even give away the coat from your back, but you couldn't restore faith and hope to a world rushing into despair.

Three days later it was decided that after all it wouldn't be necessary to engage a special accountant; the existing staff could divide the work between them, and save enlarging the salary list. Nearly three months later the ex-naval officer wrote to know whether that post or any other was still available. He could start work of any kind at any time.

Chapter Eight

The Coal Association had swelled like the Aesopian frog since its inception, and after two years it was decided that, since its scope and personnel were now greatly extended, a second organisation, bearing the awkward title of the Central Council for Economic Information, and having for its aims a purely educational economic policy, should assume independent existence, with offices of its own. It therefore took up its quarters in a fine house in Queen Anne's Gate, under a new director, a man of wide sympathies, with four heads of departments working under him. One of these was Captain V——, and another was Mr Gerard Fiennes, in charge of press activities, with whom was associated Mr W. V. Wilkins, afterwards famous for his enormously successful novel, *And So—Victoria*.

The Coal Association had been a defensive propaganda body, but the new organisation became associated with various other societies, all of them having, for their intention, the dissemination of economic facts and principles to the public in general, and in particular to the workers. It would have been easy for this to become another of the bodies for spreading the propaganda of private enterprise, but this, in fact, it never did. It survived until 1923, when it was compelled, partly through financial strain and partly because it had accomplished much of its ambition, to draw in its horns, and gradually it ceased to exist.

The new organisation was a much more comprehensive affair than its parent. It embraced almost all the industrial interests, instead of being wholly or even mainly concerned with coal. Shipping – there was a strong movement to nationalise shipping also – iron and steel and land interests, all these became involved. A glance at a committee list of that time recalls almost every great name in the industrial world. Lord Inchcape, Sir Hugh Bell, Sir Edward Ward, Sir William Noble, Lord Jersey, Lord Stanhope, Mr E. G. Pretyman (who had never been in a tram until we took him down to a debate at Bermondsey), Lord Gainford, Sir Thomas Fisher, Sir Norman Hill, Sir Alan Hutchings, Mr (now Sir Walter) Layton – those were some of the names I recall.

I never enjoyed anything as I enjoyed those committee meetings. I would have welcomed them thrice a week. These were even better than the conferences I had attended with Mr Vivian. Those had been for the making of war, these were for the making of peace. Education was their watchword. Their backers came from every political party; they could and did disagree on matters of national policy, such as reparations – there was a party in the country, by no means all socialists, who believed that the policy of reparations lay at the root of much of our unemployment – but when it came to bed-rock principles it was agreed that militarism, however successful for a time, is like the seed that fell upon a rock, that sprang up instantly, but soon, for lack of moisture, withered away. The man who is caught by your headlines this week may be 'converted' by the other chap's posters within the month. It was education, the sound grounding in economic fact, that must eventually decide the issue. It seemed to me at one time, not, I think, altogether without reason, that the fate of English industry lay in the hands of these few men gathered round a table.

Lord Inchcape was the Chairman, but my memories are chiefly of Sir Hugh Bell occupying that office. He was an old man then, but would turn up, after a long journey from his north country home, as dapper as though he had just been taken out of a bandbox. He was an elegant figure, almost thin enough to go through a napkin-ring, with a neat white beard and a knowledge of the rights and duties of a Chairman I have never seen equalled.

'You know my little weakness,' he would say to me, before the committee proceedings began. He could remember faces but not names.

I would prepare a table plan for his use, adding fresh names to the sheet he solemnly handed back to me, as new arrivals came. Now and again it happened that I did not myself know the newcomer, but I always filled in a name. Lord Northcliffe had said, 'Never tell an editor you can't do a thing.' Lord Northcliffe, I thought, was right. When dispute arose among two members as to what had actually been said, Sir Hugh quelled the tumult with a word. 'Gentlemen, we have a reporter present,' and the committee waited while I looked up the questionable passage.

Few things are more difficult, in their own way, than picking out a particular shorthand note, and I would flip desperately through the pages, looking for some distinctive outline that might act as a sign-post. While I did this, no one spoke. When at last I found it and read it aloud, Sir Hugh always assumed that my transcription was correct, and the issue stood or fell on that alone.

It was during the first year of the council's existence that I thought I might take my share in educating the public. The Press Department issued a number of weekly articles by various writers – at one time, I remember, Mr Chesterton wrote for us – and copies of these articles and of all correspondence dealing with them were sent down to the Director's Department, and the carbons filed. I always read the letters in order to be abreast of developments, and one day I saw that the author of the woman's article was resigning her agreement. Her substitute was far from satisfactory and presently she was informed that other arrangements were being made. Here, thought I, is my opportunity. I sped up to Mr Fiennes's room.

'Mr Fiennes, I see you're getting rid of your "Claudine".'

Mr Fiennes looked a little surprised. 'Yes.'

'I wonder if you would let me try my hand.'

'Have you ever done similar work?'

'No, but I'm sure I could.'

Mr Fiennes, the most courteous of men, would not have hurt the feelings of a fly. 'Send me up a specimen some time,' he suggested.

I drew one hand from behind my back. 'I've brought you *this* to show you the sort of stuff I can turn out, and *this,*' withdrawing my other hand, 'is an article that would do for next week, if you aren't already fixed up. It's a Christmas article.'

He told me to leave them both. A few days later Mr Wilkins rang down to the General Office. 'We're going to use that article of yours,' he said.

These articles were devoted to women's interests, and the idea was to conceal an economic pill in a lot of feminine jam. The opening sentence was the important one.

'Economics are like new clothes; you don't realise how fascinating they are till you get into them.'

America, with her organisations of Henpecked Husbands and similar bodies, provided plenty of opportunities to lead up to the main point. When this had been casu-ally sketched in, the article wound up with one or two sound recipes for which I had hunted through numbers of papers during the preceding week. I wrote 'Claudine' until the early part of 1923, when we began to cut down our press expenses. After the funeral bell had tolled for her I circularised all the provincial papers that had been accustomed to publish her, offering to continue this column as a personal feature. Payment from these papers was a tremendous drop from the three guineas an article I had been getting from the council, being about seven-and-sixpence a column, but the good times were over, the sands were running out, and I accepted all the offers I got at this figure, and under the name of 'Jacqueline' the articles continued for another year or so.

For some time I had been troubled about my eyes. While I was reading or working a great grey patch of mist would float in front of the eyeball, completely obscuring the print. I would wait, still as a statue, until slowly it began to move away. With this symptom came pain, becoming at last so intense that I visited an oculist.

He said, 'You have iritis.'

He was standing behind me when he spoke, and I thought he had diagnosed neuritis. Before coming to see him I had looked up an encyclopaedia, to try and discover for myself what these signs might mean and be prepared for any verdict, and I knew that neuritis was incurable, resulting in eventual total blindness.

'Oh! Neuritis,' I repeated, glad now that he was behind me.

'No, no. It's not so bad as that.' He explained. I shouldn't be able to work for some weeks, I mustn't read or even write a letter, and I must wear a dark veil whenever I went out of the house, and a black shade in it.

This was not the sort of veil used nowadays to trim hats, but a solid sheet of gauze, through which I peered uncertainly, and made me more noticed than I had ever been in my life. I wore this for months, for the attack was much more severe than we had at first supposed.

Mr Fiennes offered to make other arrangements for 'Claudine', but I assured him that I could still deliver the articles, although, until I tried, I had no notion how difficult it is to dictate one's work, particularly when the 'secretary' is a member of one's own family. My mother did all my writing for me that summer, several weeks of which we spent at the seaside. It was a very hot June, and we would bask for hours on the parade, a notable couple, I in my black veil, and she in a bath-chair, a Victorian black crinoline hat trimmed with feathers, and an open parasol. Every tract distributor for miles made a beeline for us. One old gentleman solemnly handed her a tract with a picture of the Crucifixion on the cover, saying, 'It is a wonderful thing to remember we have a Saviour who died for us.'

'Yes,' agreed my mother awkwardly, no better able than I to combat such conversation, 'isn't it?'

The old gentleman turned to me. 'Would you like a tract, too?' Clearly he thought I was suffering from some disease so frightful I dared not allow myself to be seen.

'No,' I told him firmly.

'I have several kinds,' he assured me, opening the mouth of his shiny black horsecloth satchel.

I was sure he had, including one on Salvation through Suffering.

'I can't read,' I said.

He nodded comprehendingly, and went away.

That night we added to our collection. A determined woman, clipped into a plump suit of brown tweed, strode along the parade, flinging her tracts at every person in sight. Having dumped one on my mother's lap, she separated two shy lovers on a bench, gave them a copy apiece, and went down to work her will on other couples gathered in the shadow of the breakwater. This tract described the conversion of a lady through seeing her little boy of six fall out of a window. (The tract habit is by no means dead; a few years ago I was handed one on the evils of the theatre, and only this summer someone pushed a slip into my hand – A Warning against Strong Drink – in Holland Walk, Kensington.)

It was the autumn before I was allowed to go back to the Council, and, to make up for lost time, I began my first – oh so unpublished – novel, called *Fear Goes in Sable*. It was about three hundred pages of close, single-spaced typing, with narrow margins. Its interests were human, economic, emotional, religious, and sociological. I think it contained some original verse. I typed it in a top bedroom (this was the first version; afterwards there were several others) on a typewriter so frightful that it was called Caliban. I spoke of it to no one except Joan; privately I expected it to sweep my generation and prove at least the equal of Ernest Raymond's *Tell England* that was one of the two great successes of its year.

One day, just after it was finished, but before it was typed, I woke at 2 a.m. to find my mother in a nightdress shivering beside my bed.

'Lucy,' she said, 'I'm so worried I can't sleep. It's X.' (X. was a near relative who was proposing plans of which my mother desperately disapproved.) 'I must have a cup of tea.'

I came downstairs and made the tea, and my mother talked of possible ways of compelling X. to change her plans. After a time, when she was calmer, I thought it would be wise to deflect the conversation into more exciting channels.

'Shall I tell you something?' I said.

'What is it?'

I drew a long breath. 'I have written a novel.' The words, once spoken, seemed to have all the historical importance of Queen Victoria's 'I will be good'.

'Have you, darling?' said my mother. 'How interesting. Oh, do you think we shall be able to persuade X. that it will never do?'

Ever since I left school I had been writing verses and during the last two or three years I had been selling them. Altogether I earned between £50 and £60 in this way.

They appeared in *Punch*, the *Sunday Times*, the *Observer*, and some of the literary weeklies. It was now that I received my first fan mail. It came from a lady who wrote:

Dear Sir (I signed my work with initials only), I have read some of your poems in the *Sunday Times* and elsewhere and I feel that perhaps I could help you in your career. Writing is a difficult path for the young, and as one who has trodden it for the greater part of a long life, my experience may be of use to you.

And she invited me to tea the following Sunday.

I put on my best clothes – they included a long yellow *crêpe* frock I had picked up for a guinea – and accepted the invitation. As I came into the room I was confronted by a tall woman, rigid as steel, with a determined face.

She looked me up and down. 'I thought you would be a young man of twenty-seven with golden hair,' she said.

I apologised. Neither my sex nor the colour of my hair depended upon my own choice, I assured her.

'You are envious of men?' All through our conversation she stood erect with her back to the fireplace, while I sat in an armchair and was served with the largest cup of tea I have ever seen – it must have held about a pint.

'I think, on the whole, they have a better time,' I returned, cautiously.

She shook her head. 'Oh no, my dear. In love it's much more beautiful to be a woman.'

A naturally argumentative tendency made me say, 'But they put all their eggs in one basket. It's such bad economy.'

She nodded again. 'That is true. At least, I know I always did.'

Then she told me that she believed I had a true lyric gift and a possible future. She had imagined me to be a young man, perhaps married with a young family, struggling to achieve recognition. She asked me how many poems I had had published and by whom. Then she suggested that I should make a collection and send them to a publisher, whom she named. I took her advice, and about three weeks later was able to write and say that the publisher thought my verses showed charm and delicacy of feeling, but were not sufficiently original or striking to merit publication in volume form. (Here I agreed with him.)

'Come again next Sunday and bring me EVERY-THING,' she wrote.

I wore the same yellow frock and carried a pink cardboard file. She gave me more tea, and then bid me read my verses aloud. This is an excruciating experience to any but the most brazen. When I came to one line:

> *The Moon*
> *Trailed her long cloak of silver down the street*

she interrupted me.

'Trailed her long cloak of silver down the street. That's beautiful. Go on.'

I read till my throat ached, watching her surreptitiously for signs of boredom.

When I had finished, she said: 'I have another idea. Those poems would lend themselves to illustration. You know how popular illustrated verses are.'

She was referring to the work of Mr A. A. Milne, whose 'When We Were Very Young' songs were appearing regularly in *Punch*, with illustrations by Ernest Shepard.

'Now, why not get him to illustrate your poems? Then you will easily find a publisher.'

I suggested timidly that I didn't imagine Mr Shepard would be interested. There were no rabbits or bears or little boys in my verses.

My hostess swept my objections aside. 'Everything depends on the Approach,' she said. 'Of course, you can't write in out of the blue. Now, I will tell you what I always did. I used to go and see a publisher and say, Will you give me five minutes? I will put my watch on the table, and the minute the five minutes are up, even if I am in the middle of a sentence, I will go. And, my dear, I always went. Sometimes they would follow me to the door, begging me to come back. But I never did. That is one of the great secrets of social success, to go while people still want you to stay.'

I thought perhaps I was intended to take this as a hint, and picked up my gloves. However, she paid no attention to me.

'That is what you must do,' she insisted. 'Get an appointment with Mr Shepard, take your verses with you – by the way, put on your oldest clothes. You don't want to look as though you had six hundred a year to dress on. I suppose you have something older than that?'

I was able to reassure her on that point.

'Wear it,' she said decisively, 'it may turn the scales in your favour.'

I felt logic had somehow slipped a cog. 'Why should my looking shabby make him more ready to illustrate my poems?' I asked.

'Because people like to do things to help other people, particularly when they see they need help.'

I suggested that she had got it wrong. 'Life really isn't a philanthropic affair,' I urged.

There was a lengthy pause, heavy with disapproval. At last I broke it.

'Could I not write direct to Mr Shepard, if you think it would be any good?'

'That would not be the same thing at all. Besides, what about the watch on the table? That always intrigues them.'

'It's rather like holding out a hat,' I murmured.

She folded her hands. 'Brains but no heart,' she said. 'I knew it as soon as I met you.'

This time I did stand up. 'I oughtn't to waste any more of your time,' I said awkwardly. 'I'm sorry – it's been very kind…'

She insisted on seeing me into the lift herself. A few

days later she sent me a couple of complimentary stalls for a revue, and presumably decided that that closed the account. I never heard from her again; nor did I ever go to see Mr Shepard, or have my verses published in book form.

Chapter Nine

The following Easter I found myself without a job for the first time in seven years.

The good times were over; competition in the labour market was appalling. Five pounds a week was now an unheard-of salary. Secretaries who could speak and write commercial French and German, keep books, and draw out a balance, were leaping for posts at three pounds ten. If they couldn't get them, they accepted three pounds. All the employment bureaux were dubious. Nothing attractive offered itself, and I decided to give myself a holiday.

I went down to the country, and here I attended my first and last dance. It was given by the son of a local vicar, to mark his coming of age. He had hired a neighbouring parish hall, and we all went over in cars. I had hurriedly sent home for my evening dress, that I had bought the previous year, less because I needed one than because I felt I simply couldn't go to my grave without having owned one. Since I had never danced I went into

Ipswich and took three lessons in the latest steps. When the evening came I found that, with the exception of a few of the men, I was the oldest person there. By eleven o'clock I had decided that three lessons really weren't enough.

The next morning I woke in a rage of shame, feeling I had made a fool of myself trying to dance at all. I borrowed a bicycle and rode over to Felixstowe; all the way I raged and chattered furiously to myself, so furiously that I missed the path and found myself riding down a sheep-track into a flock of sheep. At Felixstowe I got a notebook and a pencil and wrote it all down, while it was seething in my mind. When I returned to London I incorporated it in my novel.

We were leaving Auriol Road after fifteen years; during any of the last five the Sanitary Inspector could have dropped on us for the condition of the house, but one of the advantages of belonging to the middle-classes is that nobody cares about you at all. You can do what you please. It was time we left that house; actually it belonged to the mice rather more than it did to us. You found them everywhere; they chattered behind the wainscot, overran the larder, leaving their tracks everywhere; they sat on the curtain-poles and ran down the lace curtains; I had found them in the bread-tin, in the vegetable bowl, on the stairs, eating biscuit crumbs under the piano, and even occasionally in traps. There was at that time on the market a trap that killed them by drowning, and in desperation we had bought one of these. One morning, coming down early, I was perplexed by a persistent scratching and pawing close at hand. I found that a mouse had fallen into the water, and was swimming desperately round and round, trying to get some foothold for its minute claws on the smooth sides of the tank. I remembered my aunt who, finding a mouse drowning in a pail of water, had swept into the kitchen like an avenging fury, crying, 'How dare you do such a thing? Don't you know that mouse has as much right to live as you have? Yes – and more.'

I took the trap down to the garden and emptied the mouse out under the privet-bush.

We never used that trap again. When we came to take up the carpets, we found that in the dining-room the whole of the surface in one corner had been eaten away by mice. And Joan, plunging her hand into the pocket of a coat she had not worn for some time, found it full of newborn mice, hairless, ice-cold, and dead.

Finding a new home at that time was rather like searching for buried gold. You might have amazing luck, but the odds were against it. Our furniture was all of the roomy type; there was one double wardrobe so large that, with the ends knocked out, it would have made a size-able passage; but although we knew we should have to depend largely on our own efforts in keeping the house clean, we refused to be parted from our possessions.

Unquestionably we were 'choosy'. The premium era was still at its height, but we were not in a position to offer a premium. Therefore we should have been humble, but we were not. We dismissed possible houses for the most frivolous of reasons. In fact, we dismissed whole districts because my mother would suddenly decide she couldn't live in them. We would make a long journey by bus to some neighbourhood where we had been told accommodation was available, and the instant we arrived, she would say, 'Oh, this is quite impossible. I just don't like the place', and we would return on the next bus, without so much as entering a house-agent's office.

Finally, in sudden panic, she chose to take a half-house in a dubious street, several minutes' walk from station, high road, or shops. There were two rooms in that house worth the name, a huge drawing-room and a big bedroom behind it. Practically all the rest of the house was in a basement, and there was no comfort there at all. We ate our meals looking through bars, and the dustbins lived just outside the window. There was a dairy at the back and a sewing-machine overhead. Joan and I shared a big bedroom at what house-agents like to call garden level; there were bars to this window, too, and the beetles used to come in from the garden. I would find them running over the sheets, flip them on to the floor and sweep them up in a brush and pan. I couldn't kill them, so I poured them back out of the window. After Joan had gone to live in a settlement and start a career of her own, I did an enormous amount of work in this room, working late into the night. The first novel I had accepted was typed there.

That autumn I got myself another job, with a doctor this time. It was the first post I had had that I heartily disliked; I used to console myself, as I typed his letters on a non-visible typewriter (I had not known there was one left in England) and listened for the bells that rang down into the basement instead of into the room where I worked, and were just as often tradespeople as patients, with the thought that, with the labour market in its present state, I was lucky to have anything at all. Besides, had I not just despatched my book, *Fear Goes in Sable*? This job I could afford to regard as a mere temporary stopgap. It was a badly organised job; you had to bring your lunch and eat it in your room between eleven-thirty when the doctor went out and midday, when his patients began to arrive. Sometimes the patient due at twelve came at eleven-thirty. Sometimes there were so many letters there was not time to stop for food; in all the months I worked there, although I was not free until two-thirty, when I went home, and was not allowed to leave the house, neither the doctor nor his wife ever thought of sending in a cup of coffee from the dining-room. The fact was, they were terrified of their servants of whom they had three, and did not dare ask them so much as to wash an extra cup. The servants, naturally, took advantage of this. It was in this house that I heard someone telephone a coal merchant and ask if he would remove half a ton of dust and shale and bring half a ton of coal in its place.

I had been in this job no longer than two months when I heard from the first publisher to show any interest in my book, the third to whom it had been sent. This was Mr Michael Sadleir of Constables. He asked me to go and see him. I knew he was a novelist as well as a publisher and had published that spring a book with a very striking first sentence and a heroine called Viola. Its name I have forgotten. There had been an interview with him in the *Bookman* and I hunted this up and re-read it the night before I was to meet him. I also learned the names of his other books, so that I could casually introduce them into the conversation, if opportunity offered.

I was, of course, too early for my appointment and I walked up and down Orange Street until the clock chimed three. As soon as I saw him, he said, 'One day you will write a good novel, but this is not it.' He then proceeded to take my work to pieces for my benefit. I was astounded to find that all the parts of the book of which I was most proud he deplored. The bits I had expected him to condemn – the description of the typewriting office and of life in a very poor middle-class home during the war – he praised. Some of his comments I can still remember.

'Of course, this is really autobiographical, whether you realise it or not. All first novels are.'

'The quotations at the heads of the chapters are really fine.' (These, of course, were not original.)

'How old are you? Twenty-four? That's very young.' (I was so staggered by that that I could find nothing to say.)

'You know, what I can't understand is how anyone could have fallen in love with this girl.'

I insisted on taking the manuscript away in a brown-paper parcel and began rewriting it that night. No one had ever warned me that you need to be a most practised and expert author to be able to recast a book with any success. At the end of a month I sent it back to him, and within another fortnight it had been returned.

'All the original part has been deleted,' Mr Sadleir wrote. 'It was that that gave the book its flavour.'

Certainly I had dealt drastically with the heroine in the new edition. Since he had objected to her conventional outlook that, he thought, was out of character, I had now allowed her to desert her husband and elope with her lover to central Europe, where the pair immediately became involved in some conflagration in a mid-European State. Michael was killed in a brawl, while Shirley (who had improvidently given birth to a child about a year earlier) escaped on a ship that eventually went down in a magnificently described storm. The instant the ship disappeared the sea became like a floor of black glass. I thought it was a striking close; after all, the three would now be reunited for eternity.

The day after it came back from Constables I sent it to Fisher Unwins. After a suitable lapse of time I received an invitation to go to that office and discuss it. Mr Unwin was himself in conference, but I saw two members of his staff.

'You have the makings of a novelist,' said one of them,

'but you haven't quite rung the bell this time. We'd like to see anything else you write, though. We think you show a lot of promise.'

I asked, perplexed, 'What actually is wrong with the book?'

He replied, 'It's on the depressing side, don't you think? I mean – all those deaths in the last chapter.'

'Depressing! Why, that's my idea of a cheerful ending.'

'The public wouldn't agree with you,' said my companion gently. 'We have to consider Box Office a little.'

Quite undaunted, I said, 'Well, perhaps I could rewrite it, with a different end.'

'Send it back to us, if you do,' he suggested. 'There's no hurry, you know. How soon do you think you would get it done?'

'Oh, June, say.' I didn't wish to sound too eager. It was now February.

'Well, remember we shall be here in July or even August. Give yourself time.'

I can't think why I left that office absolutely convinced that my future as a novelist was assured.

Meanwhile, while this book was tossing about among the publishers, I had produced another. It happened this way.

The King's Theatre was comparatively close and my mother and I went to see *Cat and the Canary* one Saturday night. It was a marvellous play, hands coming out of wall panels to clutch pearl necklaces from the necks of lovely sleeping girls, fireplaces swinging inwards and elderly men vanishing without a sound, all the bundle, in fact. The excitement did not wane for an instant. Nevertheless, stirring the breakfast porridge next day, I observed to Joan, 'I believe I could do as well as that.'

'Well, why don't you?' she suggested, sensibly.

'All right,' I promised. 'I'll give myself six weeks.'

I think I was rather surprised when, at the end of six weeks, the book was finished. I sent it to Collins, thinking, 'A detective novel will be a nice change for them.' Actually, it was only a detective novel in the sense that it contained a murder; it had several original touches, I thought, and the murderer escaped to live a useful life elsewhere. After the usual six weeks, the usual thing happened; I was asked to call and see the publishers. The general manager told me that, if I would revise certain points, he would recommend publication. By that time I was interested in another book and was inclined to be cool about this one, but as soon as I got home I set about altering it. The book was now accepted on the publishers' usual terms for first novels.

I was wild with excitement at having a book taken, but once again was disappointed in the terms. I had supposed that an advance of £200 would be a reasonable offer on account of royalties, but I was later assured that £40 was handsome for a book by an unknown writer. Anyway, the book failed to earn even this sum, being a complete flop. I was tragic about this. I couldn't understand it. I decided, like every unsuccessful author since time began, that it had not had its fair share of advertisement. Subsequently I wrote another, that Collins refused on the grounds that the plot was unsound, but they hoped I would try again. I felt that I was now, as an author, permanently discredited. No one could conceivably live down this double failure. I no longer wanted to talk about books.

One of the main disappointments of this was that it drove me back to office life. Offices weren't fun any more, they were loathsome. However, I found myself some political work, on the Conservative side, that was not without interest. My working day began immediately after lunch and might go on till midnight. I enjoyed going to the House of Commons and being recognised by the policeman at St Stephen's Gate. I liked to hear the policemen inside shouting the names of the members as they came down to interview individual constituents. Once I even filled in a card and interviewed one on my own account. A good deal of my work was done outside the office; I would go to look up facts at the headquarters of the Conservative Association; or I would be sent to verify some rumour that was floating about ten years earlier, at the office of one of the most obscure journals, usually of colonial origin.

In the office I wrote letters on hotel paper and signed them with a pseudonym, and some of these appeared in papers like the *Financial Times*. One of the subjects in which 'we' were interested was the proposed tax on tea. This was, I think, in the year 1925. I went to the first Wembley Exhibition and wrote it up for some Far Eastern papers. 'A Woman's View of Wembley' it was called. Out of the money allotted to me for expenses I bought a fine lunch and two consecutive rounds on the Giant Racer. Using my employer as an introduction I went behind the scenes and talked to the men in charge of some of the pavilions.

When that work came to an end I got myself a temporary post at the University of London. It was the sort of clerk's work I used to hand out to typists when I was twenty, and I was paid a typist's wage – 50s. a week. When I was alone I would sometimes cry with humiliation. But I was like the dipsomaniac who cannot forsake his bottle. I began a new detective story, and finished it in three months. By the time it was done I was again out of work. Fifty shillings a week is not much but it enables you to keep your head above water; on the other hand, it gives you no opportunity to save. I answered numbers of advertisements of every kind, but I had no replies, or none that were any use. Now and again I would keep an appointment, but at one office I was told frankly that they preferred girls of a different social class and another seemed to me so humiliating that as soon as I left the office I turned into a post-office and sent a card, saying I had had to change my plans and could no longer consider the post.

My peak hours were eight in the morning and nine at night, when the postman called. As the days went on I felt like someone walking between high walls, looking desperately ahead and finding no break anywhere. Now and again I would sell some verses for thirty shillings or two guineas, but that was all. Meanwhile I finished my book. I was so unsure of myself that I didn't even know whether it was good of its kind or not. I titled it easily enough, but was perplexed about the signature. I could not damn its chances out of hand by using the first very pseudonymous pseudonym. Anyway, I had decided to take a man's name this time. I found there were still plenty of people who didn't believe in women as writers of crime stories. This was before Dorothy Sayers or the author of *The Murder of Roger Ackroyd* had arrived to head the list of detective authors.

I decided at length to call myself Michael Scott, from my favourite 'Lay of the Last Minstrel'.

> *In these far climes it was my lot*
> *To meet the wondrous Michael Scott;*
> *A wizard of such dreaded fame*
> *That, when, in Salamanca's cave,*
> *Him listed his magic wand to wave,*
> *The bells would ring in Notre Dame!*

Unfortunately a man of this name had written a book called *Tom Cringle's Log*, so reluctantly I abandoned that notion. I thought I would cling to Scott, so I chose the first name Gilbert, which seemed (and seems) to me a sissy-sounding sort of name, and the kind a woman has a right to, if she likes. Gilbert Scott then. Short and easy to remember. But happening to open the telephone book a few days before the typing of the manuscript, I found no fewer than three Gilbert Scotts. So that name had to be abandoned, too. I was resolved to stick to Gilbert. And then I remembered Gerald du Maurier, who was my idol of the theatre, who had appeared in a play called *The Dancers*, in which he answered to Tony. Tony then – or rather, Anthony, since Tony was reminiscent of Kiwi, the toney boot polish.

Anthony Gilbert. I typed the name on the manuscript, and then wondered how I could camouflage my identity with my agent. After my earlier failures I felt very sensitive about letting him know who Gilbert really was. Among some papers I found a single headed sheet of very thick, very expensive notepaper that had belonged to the family's redoubtable Uncle George – stamped with the crest, a leg in armour with the French motto, *Toujours Prêt*. It bore an address in Cromwell Road, but it was easy to scratch this out and write, in a magnificently disguised hand, Temporary Address: 45 Sinclair Road. Then I planned the letter.

Dear Sirs,
A mutual friend has given me your name. I enclose herewith the manuscript of a crime novel entitled ———. I shall be glad to know your opinion of this. I have been assured that Messrs. Collins stand high in the ranks of publishers of this type of fiction. I am myself too much out of

touch with contemporary publishers to offer any alternative suggestion. The above address will find me for the present.

And then an unforgettable, almost indecipherable, but exceedingly characteristic signature.

No one pierced the disguise. I received a polite letter within the week, approving my novel and assuring me that it should be submitted to Collins immediately. Before there was time to hear their verdict, however, I had discovered a new author, a man called Michael Arlen, who had written a book of short stories, called *These Charming People*. I was entranced by them. Instantly I invented a character who should emulate Mr Arlen's style. His name was Sebastian Sanjoy, and he was, like Saul, a mighty man of valour, with the head of a pirate and a tossing golden beard. He was, of course, a villain, but after the Robin Hood manner. Only he went one better than that national hero. He robbed the rich – true – but with such charm that he was forgiven, although he had only his own advantage at heart.

I submitted two stories – and waited a week. At the end of this time I received a letter saying that the style of the stories was vaguely reminiscent of a writer called Arlen, although the matter was original. Could the author do anything about it? The author, an obliging fellow, thought he could. They were rewritten and sent back. Another week passed. Then a telephone call came from the London University. A voice I detested said, 'I daresay you'd be glad of a little work, wouldn't you?'

I dared not refuse. If I only worked for a fortnight it was five pounds, and the winter was coming on, and all the expenses of warm coats and shoes. I reported at the University next morning at ten o'clock. I had been working for about a week, when yet another letter came. My posts were exciting those days, more exciting, I fancy, than they have ever been since; or perhaps the novelty wears off. Anyway, this letter said:

Dear Mr Gilbert,
If you can call and see me tomorrow afternoon, you may, as the advertisements say, hear something to your advantage.

And it was signed Nancy Pearn.

I rang up, passionate with anxiety. Could she wait at the office until six? I could not get away before half-past five. Miss Pearn obligingly could. When I reached the office she told me that the *Sketch* (the shiny-papered weekly *Sketch*) had taken both my stories and wanted four more to complete the series. They offered sixty-five pounds for the lot.

Sixty-five pounds! That represented six months' work at the University. I went back, and that night I sat up plotting a new story. A few days later I heard that Collins would publish the Anthony Gilbert novel. They asked for some publicity material, an interview and a photograph.

The first of these was easy to manufacture. Who knew anything about Mr Gilbert? Nobody, not even Mr Gilbert himself. Eventually he figured as a retiring sort of chap, whose hobbies were breeding Scotch terriers on the Sussex Downs and photographing ancient churches. As to the interviews, the agents said that Mr Gilbert was seldom in town, so Collins waived that. But the photograph was a more serious affair, and presented obvious difficulties.

I had not, however, been brought up in a good home for nothing. I knew, therefore, having been taught this since childhood, that difficulties are made to be solved. A dozen years later I knew that if you wanted any kind of theatrical properties, they could be hired from Messrs. Nathans without any trouble, but in 1926 I scarcely even knew the name. Instead, I went to the hairdressing department of the Army and Navy Stores, and inquired, 'Do you stock wigs and beards?'

'Only to order,' replied the grave lady in charge of the department.

'Then could you order one of each for me?'

It is, apparently, impossible to disconcert heads of departments. 'We shall have to take your measurements. Will you take off your hat?'

An enthralling conversation ensued. As to the wig – what shade? Where parting? Covering or not covering ears?

My ears had once been praised. Not covering the ears, then. Parting? Middle. Colour? A good middle-aged colour. Not marcelled, of course, but luxuriant. When it came to the beard, it seemed there was yet more choice. Beards could be spade, pointed, the all-over that dispenses with the necessity of a shirt, the divided, seen most often in religious paintings, or the Frenchman's tip. I decided on a good square beard – because one never knows. Say what you like, women's figures aren't the same as men's, more bumpy altogether, and here as in so many other things, I have a leaning towards Victorianism. So a full beard and moustache were ordered, I paid five-and-sixpence and went away to wait for another week.

When they arrived both wig and beard proved to be on the generous scale. I pinned back my shingle, fitted on the wig, covered the obvious parting with a borrowed Homburg hat, adjusted the hooks of the beard over my ears, and wondered if it might not have been wiser to have used a French name. Because, although beards were beginning to struggle back into the mode, even Chelsea at that time could hardly offer anything so blatant, so triumphant as this beard. Even Sebastian Sanjoy's can hardly have been its equal. However, all the best people are born to suffer, and it won't last long. Into a taxi-cab steps a peculiar figure, clad as to its upper portions in gentleman's attire, but, in place of the anticipated trousers, a rather elongated kilt – my modest blue skirt, reaching in the year 1926 a little way below the knee.

Presumably photographers, like doctors, cannot be surprised. Three poses were taken, the last minus a hat. This picture, however, was unsuccessful; the parting was

so strongly marked it might have been stitched in silk on
the proof itself. One of the others, however, was more
successful. Certainly there was little to link up the Lucy
her family knew, apple-cheeked, smooth-skinned, wearing rimless pince-nez, with this benevolent Germanic
professor in tortoise-shell horners. He looked, indeed, in
his benevolence and innocence – for the combination of
that thickly grown beard and the entire absence of lines
in the face produced an aspect of almost unearthly purity
– not altogether unlike Louisa M. Alcott's Professor Bhaer.
All the same, the picture was not destined for publication,
the agents pointing out that the publishers are under the
impression they have discovered a new, vigorous, young
author, who will continue to enchant (or bore) his public
for many years, and that to present them with an elderly
gentleman with one toe feeling precariously for the rim
of the tomb might have unfortunate effects on future
contracts. That was a pity, but I am not Yorkshire (with
a dash of Scotch) for nothing. At least, I resolved, the
photograph should not be wasted. So, as soon as I had a
room of my own, up it went on the mantelpiece. It was
a large, not to say, an imposing picture. It was difficult to
overlook, and indeed it never was overlooked. Curious
female friends and relatives, all of them secretly intrigued
at a woman having a 'study', inspected it minutely.

'Who is that, my dear?'

Lucy (modestly), 'Oh, just someone I know.'

'A writer?' Only ink or paint could excuse a beard of
those proportions.

Lucy, 'Yes.'

A pause. Then the inevitable female question. 'Is he married?'

Lucy (very gently), 'Not happily,' obeying Mr Somerset Maugham's dictum that a person who is not married at all cannot be happily married.

And there the mystery remained for some years. I offered no explanations; my mother offered none. The visitors were clearly a bit dubious. This writing business, now ... After all, where has it led to date? One book that nobody wanted to read. Why not take up needlework or nursing or some *womanly* profession? Besides, said those intelligent glances, we married women know all about these unhappily married men. And not, so far as one can judge from the picture, an Englishman, even. I'm sorry some instinct, later on, made me destroy that photograph. In its way it was a masterpiece.

Collins thought nothing of the carefully prepared 'publicity'. Who, they presumably inquired, is going to be interested in a new author whose acknowledged amusements are dogs and churches? A publisher can go several better than that. And so, in the spring of 1927, this sort of thing appeared in a number of London and Colonial newspapers:

Since Scott set the fashion with the Waverley novels, books by pseudonymous writers have often been remarkably successful. The latest 'mystery' author is Mr Anthony Gilbert, whose clever first detective novel *The Tragedy at Freyne* has just been published by Collins. His identity has been closely guarded and the publishers themselves do not know his real name. For a time J. D. Beresford was suspected of having ventured into the detective field, and Archibald Marshall was also credited with its authorship. Meanwhile, connoisseurs of detective stories are trying to fathom the mystery of the suspiciously mature 'first' novel which betrays a skilled hand in dramatic situations.

I should like to suggest that 'Anthony Gilbert' conceals the identity of a well-known amateur airman who is already popular as a writer on other themes and has played a fairly prominent part in the political world for many years. – *Cassell's Weekly*.

This subsequently appeared in a number of other papers. There are no two ways about it – when it comes to publicity you have to hand it to the publishers every time.

The book was comparatively well received. Rose Macaulay praised it; the *Liverpool Post* said, 'The deduction is brilliant, the best of its kind since *Trent's Last Case.*' *Cassell's Weekly* said it was of that quality that all readers of Mr Gilbert's previous novels would readily anticipate; the *Glasgow Herald* considered it daringly original and compared it with Gaboriau; *John o' London* called it a brilliant detective story; the *Sunday Times* recommended it; the *New York Times* followed suit; even the *Spectator* could 'point no flaw in the chain of events'.

Mr Gilbert felt that, unlike his poor relation of a year or two back, he had made an auspicious beginning. No doubt the foreign reviews, of which there were several, were equally congratulatory, but unhappily nobody could translate them.

Presumably when the second book appeared, the author thought he might lend a hand. The papers say:

> Messrs. Collins are still in the dark as to the identity of one of their detective authors, Mr Anthony Gilbert, whose clever first novel, etc., etc. The author writes: 'As you are doubtless aware, Anthony Gilbert is a pseudonym, and has thus far successfully concealed the name that would be well known to yourself and others. I am sorry that I cannot let you have my photograph, as this would effectually give the show away.'

Is it the writer's fault if the publishers should conclude from this disarming confession that the author is, at least, a member of the Cabinet or sits on the Bishops' Bench? As for 'well known', presumably publishers recall, though no one else does, the names of their authors whose books have failed? (You will remember that the first ill-starred effort was offered to the public by the same house?)

Again the book was well noticed, although the most terse review came from America:

Déclassée beauty found strangled in Pontifex Mansions, Bloomsbury, clutching three short black hairs … A blackmailing plot relating to a murder in the past, amorous intrigues among the leading persons, gaily dressed scenes, sufficient suspense and real interest are among the ingredients of a tale teaching that old sins have long shadows, that what always happens is the last thing you'd expect, and that Anthony Gilbert is a safe bet *pour passer le temps*.

The last quotation comes from a Canadian paper, who doesn't see why the old country should have all the fun:

All that Mr Lincoln MacVeagh of the Dial Press knows is that Anthony Gilbert is a name assumed by one of the most popular British novelists, who does not want his identity known when he turns his hand to detective fiction. Many guesses have been made as to the true name of the mysterious 'Mr Gilbert' and these guesses run all the way from Hugh Walpole to May Sinclair.

After that, interest in Mr Gilbert regrettably died down, though he still had an occasional triumph. At the Crime Club luncheon, inaugurated by Foyles, limelight was played on all the authors present, and when Anthony Gilbert rose to his feet there was a roar of laughter all over the room. A young man leaped from an adjacent table.

'Are you really Anthony Gilbert?'

'I really am.'

'You know, when I tell my wife she'll never believe me. We've neither of us ever thought of you as a woman.'

That was Mr Philip Johnson, the journalist and playwright.

Chapter Ten

Nineteen twenty-six was the end of the second epoch, the epoch of wage-earning in offices. At the end of that year we warehoused our furniture and went into seaside lodgings. All through the autumn I had searched hopelessly for some flat or maisonette at a reasonable rent, but there were difficulties. My mother's illness was now the governing factor in all our decisions; stairs were a great difficulty, she disliked lifts, her map of London was still a good deal more circumscribed than that of most people. The only ground-floor flat that seemed at all possible was on Ealing Common, but there were thorns even among these roses. There was a baby in the basement who would shout, if not squall, under the drawing-room window; the drawing-room itself, owing to some structural deficiency, was under water; six rooms had been made by the simple expedient of running up partitions, and making a flat out of two large rooms and a lobby. The mouldings of the ceilings stopped dead at the new walls, and were continued in the next room. The mantelpieces were huge and of heavily veined marble. Worst of all, the house-agents were so lackadaisical they did not know a thing about the ownership of the garden, the extent of tenant's liabilities or even the length of the lease. So we wrote to Mr Pope of Hammersmith to call for the furniture and went down to Westcliff, where we stayed a good deal longer than we had intended.

Westcliff was the nearest seaside town to London; it had a good train service; the air was well spoken of. Also it is untrue to say, as many do, that there is no sea at Westcliff; there is as much sea at Westcliff (and Southend) as there is at Hastings, Brighton, or Eastbourne. Certainly it goes out a very long way, so far that if you are only rushing through the town you may not even glimpse it; but it comes the whole way back.

Westcliff is built on a hill; my mother could, by this time, only go out in a bath-chair. Indeed, except for a few journeys to town to buy carpets, after we had settled at our next house, I do not remember her ever going out in any other way. These chairs were hired locally, and we obtained permission to keep one in the hall overnight; first thing in the morning it was wheeled out on to the path. The difficulty about bath-chairs and hills will be obvious. Steering a not very light weight, it is difficult not to go downhill too fast, or to get uphill at all. And everything at Westcliff, except the sea itself, is at the back of the town. Even the churches are a mile away.

That was a snowy Christmas, with the snow lying in great drifts before the municipal authorities had time to clear it away, and one's galoshes came off on the way to church on Christmas morning, and had to be retrieved from a snow-pile. It was the first Christmas no one came down – not even Joan, who had achieved 'independence' in the shape of a furnished bed-sitting-room at the top of a little house off Holland Road, a small room facing west, with a tunnel to the window. We all seem to have been rather cramped for space that winter. Our furnished sitting-room was small, and contained a narrow writing-desk, upon whose ledge with care it was possible to balance the 'new' second-hand typewriter that had replaced the detestable Caliban, a small curly red plush sofa and two stiff armchairs to match, three table chairs, and a sideboard. Work had to stop sharp at ten out of deference to the other boarders. In this room we lived, ate, worked, and read for eight months. Joan was our only visitor; she came whenever she could, wearing a dashing new red wool jersey suit from Peter Jones, the *dernier cri* in chic. And once she brought the friend with whom, later, she was to share a flat for five years. No one else came, naturally. London seemed as remote as the North Pole.

Southend, the tripper's Paradise, presents in winter an appearance of death. Once the season has begun there are teashops and cafés all along the parade; in the central street, running down to the sea, stalls sell milk, whelks, books, cups of tea, ice-cream cornets, spades and pails, shrimping nets, rubber bloomers for the baby, bathing suits and slips, straw hats, walking-sticks, films – then it is the hub of activity. But in January, when we made our first excursion there, wheeling the chair along the front, these stalls did not exist. It is only possible to realise the extent of activities in summer by reading the names painted over the shops. Everyone as far as the eye can reach sells eatables. But at the beginning of the year, with the cold sea slapping against the stones, it was like a city of the dead. The train service, too, for those who did not take the 'business gents' specials, was disappointing. The return fare to London was six shillings, and the special trains at reduced rates intolerably slow. Besides, they only ran on certain days.

Living at the seaside brings its own reflections. What a pity, for instance, in this inventive age, that a seafront should still only extend in two directions. If only it could offer more diversions; but it can't be helped. Before lunch you wheel the chair into Southend, and after lunch in the direction of Leigh-on-Sea. When these entertainments pall, there is the town, but that involves climbing over the railway. Still, it all makes a change.

One of my naval cousins married while we were at Westcliff, and my father and I went to the wedding. There were plenty of local dress shops – it did not occur to us that the occasion might warrant a day in town – but the choice was narrow. It is symbolic of my sartorial taste at that time that I appeared at the wedding in a black *crêpe* frock, with a pink georgette collar and minute gilt buttons, a fawn-coloured coat, and a 'shape' covered in coffee-coloured georgette and trimmed with

an upstanding spray in orange and gold. Joan arrived in
a ravishing confection of green, costing more guineas
than one had ever believed it possible to pay for a frock,
and a two-guinea hat that remained the wonder of the
family for years to come. Of the wedding I remember
chiefly an aunt in a daring black satin confection, and
champagne that was, somehow, a disappointment. Also
that the Bishop, now permanently returned from the
Cannibal Islands, was very much in evidence.

In the spring, when the new book had been finished
and despatched, the hunt for a flat began again. I used to
come up on a cheap ticket and, since by now it seemed
to be accepted that we were going to live in Ealing,
I would book a ticket to the Common and make my
round of the familiar house-agents. There were plenty
of flats to be had; for the most part these would be
one floor of two-storey houses, at rents approximating
to £160 a year. Frequently these were not self-contained;
often it was part of the contract that you should take over
carpets and curtains. At last one agent said, 'I suppose you
would not consider a house. We have a delightful house
to let in Gordon Road.'

Gordon Road, as all lovers of Ealing know, is that
endless highway stretching from Haven Green to West
Ealing. The house we were offered and eventually took
was half-way down. It is amazing, now, the way in which
we swallowed the bait. Certainly, from outside, it seemed
an improvement on anything we had had for years, and

my father used to say it was the best house we ever had. But then he didn't have the running of it. Nor did the man who designed it. Architects seem, in the main, to be born without sense or any bowels of compassion. The kitchen quarters were dark as a dungeon and large as the average town flat for two people. There were twelve doors in this part of the house alone. The first led from the hall into a minute lobby, furnished with hooks; the second opened into the pantry, with a sink and tall shelves and cupboards full of meters; the third went into the great barren kitchen, looking on to a blank wall and perpetually dark, a barn of a place with a huge dresser, an old-fashioned kitchen range, and more cupboards; the fourth took you into the scullery, where there was a gas-cooker and another sink and shelves for saucepans, so high they were never dusted or cleaned; a fifth, on the left, introduced the larder; a sixth took you, *en route*, to the seventh, which opened into the 'slype', a long covered passage where bicycles could be kept, and ladders slung on the walls. The eighth opened into a shed (more bicycles, gardening tools, folding chairs, all the flotsam and jetsam of an incurably hoarding household). The ninth led to the coal-cellar, the tenth to the big north garden; the eleventh opened on to the passage bordered by the wall that made the kitchen so dark, and where the dustbins were kept, and the twelfth led to the back door gate.

The whole place was far too big for three people, of whom one was an invalid, particularly in view of the fact that servants were hard to come by and my mother would never employ local labour. During the next three years our staff consisted of an erratic 'daily help' from Shepherds Bush, who came, in good weeks, for two whole and two half-days and in bad weeks not at all. At Christmas she was always away for three to four weeks, and at that season it was impossible even to get the steps cleaned; the private hotels absorbed every one remotely employable. On the ground floor were three sitting-rooms, two of them enormous, a big square hall and a passage leading to the garden; on a mezzanine floor was the worst designed bathroom I ever have seen (with all the space at his disposal the architect never seems to have spared more than a couple of minutes for essential services), a huge shabby box-room, fitted with shelves (you could have furnished a mausoleum with the shelves in that house), and a servant's bedroom. Upstairs again were five more rooms, of which one looked over the blank passage and was dark all the year round. Of these five one became my workroom. I had never had a room of my own before, and certainly it was an advantage not to have to shuffle the papers together and cover up the typewriter when it was time to set the cloth for lunch.

No one gave a thought to the carpeting and linoleum such a monster of a house would demand; it was a roof and it was escape from Westcliff where, it seemed, one might moulder into dust before anything happened to break the monotony. We arranged to move in at the end of the June quarter, but a smoke test revealed the fact that the drains were in an impossible condition, and would have to be renewed before the house could again be lived in. Which was why we spent Bank Holiday at Southend.

This famous town wakes up, briefly, for the Easter weekend, then shuts down into immobility until the end of June. From the middle of July until early in September the place is a never-closed Fun Fair. Bank Holiday was an unforgettable spectacle, quite unfamiliar, quite un-English. The public gardens were packed with Jews; plump Jewesses in black satin, fitting very snugly, with black hats like turbans, sat on the public benches, reading papers in Yiddish; you heard the unfamiliar language on all hands. Shops hung out signs 'Kosher Cooking here' and all the tables were full. Picnic parties flooded on to the beach, with bathing-dresses, baskets, and thermos flasks; scarcely a stone could be seen. Sometimes you wondered how it was they didn't feed the wrong face. On the sand stood an old man, looking like one of the prophets of the Old Testament; he had a beard that would not have disgraced Mr Gilbert, and he carried sandwich-boards and a bundle of tracts.

'The wicked shall be turned into hell...While we were yet sinners Christ Jesus died for the ungodly,' those boards proclaimed. When the crowds went away the beach was thick with tracts, bottles, paper bags, and empty cigarette packets. The mile-and-a-quarter pier for which Southend is justly famous was thronged with human-ity; people waited in queues at the automatic machines. There were pierrot shows, musical shows, individual

performers; men lined the parade selling balloons, whiz-
zers, coloured paper hats, spades, rolls that squeaked and
joke cigars. Whelks were twopence a plate – five to a
portion – forks and vinegar thrown in. Winkles are eaten
by all manner of people, but whelks are an acquired
taste. They have a peculiarly tough leathery substance;
that day a pair of false teeth got stuck in a particularly
stubborn whelk, and both teeth and whelk had to be
removed and fought apart before an admiring audience.
The bath-chair threaded its way through this storm of
humanity at a funeral pace. Flags of every nation and of
none waved on sand-castles; the breakwaters were black
with holiday crowds. I forget how many people had
slept on the beach, because lodgings were not available;
you couldn't put a car or a bicycle at a garage within a
couple of miles. Tram-cars and omnibuses were choc-
a-bloc. And when evening came the queues from the
station stretched all down the road. Up the street after
dinner, making their way back to the charabancs, went
youths and girls in big parties, shouting music-hall hits.
Dancing went on until all hours. At no time during the
day was it possible to get a place on a seat on the front.
The instant any one stirred there was a vigilant watcher
ready to pounce.

The day after the Bank Holiday the municipal authorities sent out an army to clear the shore and the public
places. Compared with yesterday it was quiet, but all day
the charabancs came thundering into Southend, rooms
all round, at Westcliff and Leigh-on-Sea, were packed.

The season was in full swing when we left at last, in the middle of August, to 'take up residence' in Gordon Road, Ealing.

My mother's first comment on the new house, which she had not hitherto seen, was that the rooms were on the small side. Only when we came to carpet them and found that none would take a carpet less than twelve feet by ten feet six inches did she change her mind. We had our first meal in the uncarpeted drawing-room – new bread and butter and potted turkey and tongue, and the inevitable tea – while the workmen, who had barely finished even now, sat on packing-cases on the lawn and ate their more robust meal. We only had one carpet, which went down in the dining-room. For the rest, there was a mat or two which we carried into whichever room we were for the moment using. There had been some misunderstanding with the powers that be and the electric current had not been switched on. We sent my father out to buy candles, and did the best we could.

Settling down presented more difficulties than it ever does when I move house these days. I would be ashamed to move in and not have the place shipshape before going to bed; but then there was so much more furniture, so many more knick-knacks, hundreds and hundreds of books for which we no longer have house-room. The next day the work of furnishing began in earnest; we bought a Persian carpet for the huge north drawing-room – a room that clamoured for something cosy in rose – and made up for this sobriety by having

rose shades to the lights. This room was papered in a
dead white satin-stripe, and all the familiar furniture
came here. Did we bring the piano to Gordon Road? I
cannot be sure, but I believe we did. Certainly we had
the piano-stool, full of music which no one ever played,
and with a leg that collapsed without warning whenever anyone sat down. There was a sofa, too, in 'French'
tapestry, across whose decrepit and bulging springs at
reasonable intervals we nailed strips of webbing; it had an
adjustable head and was buttoned all over. The armchairs
were covered in a sensible mud-coloured corduroy, that
'went with everything'; there was an octagonal rosewood
table, supporting photograph frames, silver spoons and
matchboxes, and a number of books in *suède* bindings –
Canon Holmes's *Story of the Months* and *Story of the Days*,
in green and blue respectively, Ella Wheeler Wilcox in
pale green leather, *Omar Khayyam* in white vellum tied
with yellow ribbon, a tiny and entrancing book about
an inch long and almost as wide, called *The Adventures
of Dot*, enhanced by minute illustrations coloured by an
earlier generation, several badges of the Primrose League
(inherited from Uncle George); while a second and
smaller rosewood table was covered with family photographs and a huge terracotta jar with a dragon design,
for ornamental purposes only. The rosewood escritoire,
the ebony corner cupboard, the bookcase full of large
red morocco volumes – Reading from Great Literature
– all these lined the walls and were dominated, as they
had been dominated in every house in turn, by the

whatnot, an enormous bamboo construction, furnished with drawers and cupboards and inset mirrors and little brackets and shelves, inlaid with gilt birds and leaves, and covered with china ornaments and brass dishes and bits of ivory and jade, and a leather cigar-case from Japan, an old Chelsea teapot (relic of my father's bachelor days, when he bought it for five shillings from his landlady) and a box of Charles Kingsley's complete works in a box with a badly burned back. Inside the cupboards were the family photographs we didn't care to have on view and the old family scrap albums, fascinating affairs full of tiny coloured pictures and transfers and cards with lace edges and carefully copied verses in a pale brownish ink, with long s's and immaculate handwriting. Of these only one now remains, like a bit of forgotten family history. All the pictures here were water-colours in gilt frames, executed by dead and gone relatives.

And after the carpets came the purchase of curtains. Each window was shrouded in lace curtains reaching to the floor. When buying these, you sat upright on chairs in John Barker's showroom and an obliging shopman flung each pattern over a brass rail so that you could observe the 'fall'. We were very 'choosy' about our patterns; nothing in the nature of cupids or urns or birds of paradise, but mighty scrolls and bold flower designs, where roses and water-lilies improbably intertwined, usually won the day. The windows of this house were all very wide; some of the largest took two pairs of lace curtains, hung in symmetrical pleats. Although the war had introduced a new fashion for window-dressing, coloured curtains that pulled right across, giving the room a warm and intimate look at night, we remained loyal to the ancient tradition of long coloured curtains at the sides, looped back on to brass hooks, with ribbon bows or plush tasselled cords, and long yellow blinds to shut out the gaze of the curious. And we had 'frills' – not pelmets, but yards and yards of material strung on pieces of tape and hung across the top of the window to conceal the pins. For we stuck to curtain poles – not for us the modern 'railways' or those delightful wires you buy at Woolworth's and adjust to your need. All the coloured curtains were made by hand, without a machine. They reached from curtain pole to floor, and involved days of backbreaking labour. We calculated, later, how many yards of material had been sewn. It worked out at about twenty yards per room, allowing for seams.

The hall, the stairs, the landing, and the kitchen quarters were all covered by home labour. Stair carpet and linoleum were sent home in rolls and laid by oneself.

'And when would it be convenient for the men to call?' the shopman would ask politely, pencil poised.

'We shall not require it laid,' my mother would say quietly. This was not because of the expense, in the main, but because 'I don't care for workmen about the house and I am sure you can manage', my mother would say.

Now, laying linoleums is a skilled job; first of all, you need an expert with a pencil and a measure to make out a plan; then you need another expert to cut the lengths so that they will fit snugly round the newel-post of the bannisters, and the kitchen range. And certainly it is not a job to be tackled between breakfast and the time to put on the potatoes for lunch. That, however, was when I tackled it.

Laying the kitchen linoleum was perfectly bloody or a grand joke, according to the way you looked at it. The kitchen was enormous; even if you possessed skill, time and patience, there was no area in the house large enough to spread out that roll and cut the pieces as they should be cut, and fitted together. The kitchen, owing to its doors, dresser and cupboard, to say nothing of the range, was a series of angles. After an hour and a half of contriving this and that, a visitor, peering through the door into that dungeon, would have seen nothing but a vast roll of lino, apparently miraculously suspended in space. Further investigation would have revealed the author, prone on her back on the boards, the roll held aloft, one hand stabbing frantically with a linoleum cutter at the stubborn underside. Even if you do not suffer from astigmatism (as I do) it is not easy to cut linoleum in a straight line, in that position. But what alternative was there? Of course, there may be dozens, but I could conceive none. When matters were at their most ticklish – and it is amazing how a whole morning flies past when you are really engrossed – a voice called from the head of the staircase, 'Is my lunch coming soon, dear? It's a quarter past one.'

Feeling like a rather disreputable troglodyte, I crawled

out. (This is harder than it sounds, when you are encased in linoleum like a moth in a chrysalis.)

'It may be a little late,' I apologised, 'but it won't be long.'

The truth was I had forgotten, in the fascination of my task, that food existed. Some people have minds like Mr Arlen's hero, that was like Clapham Junction and went all ways at once, and some only have a single-track affair that cannot concentrate in more than one direction at a time.

Lunch was fried lemon sole, *purée* of potatoes, and cauliflower with a cream sauce. No pudding because of the linoleum. If you cut potatoes into small pieces and 'gallop' them, straining them before they are quite cooked, shaking them dry, and then creaming them with butter and milk, you can cook them in a quarter of an hour. The bits that even a silver fork cannot break up can be left behind in the colander. The important part of a cauliflower is the heart; no invalid is going to wonder whether the stalk is cooked or not, because invalids don't eat stalks; as for the fish, that takes no time at all. Just whisk up an egg, dip the fillets, roll them in breadcrumbs, put them into steaming fat; put on a kettle for the hot-water plate, melt a nut of butter for the sauce, stir in a little flour, add the milk, and leave it on one side until you can give it your undivided attention. Because, if it is left unstirred for a moment, it goes lumpy. While the vegetables 'come to the boil', lay a table upstairs, for we are lunching on the top floor today.

'How's the linoleum getting on?'

'I think it's going to look fine.'

'How long before lunch?'

'Oh, no time at all now.'

The actual dishing up of even a simple meal really needs four or five hands; the potatoes must be made into a *purée*, the cauliflower drained, the sauce stirred, the plate filled, the fish freed of the smallest trace of grease; then push everything at lightning speed on to the butler's tray, negotiate what was an hour or so earlier a promising roll of linoleum, guide the tray up the two flights of stairs, and all is well. The fish had not burnt, the sauce was not lumpy, the vegetables passed muster. And in spite of subsequent pots of tea, and the washing-up to be done, and a tray laid for afternoon tea, by one of those miracles that cannot be explained, the linoleum was all laid by four o'clock, and looking quite as professional as was necessary. Thanks to the enormous steel fender that had followed us faithfully from Norwood to West Kensington, thence to Sinclair Road and now, from the warehouse to Ealing, the place where the knife (or one's eye) slipped was not really noticeable. Everyone agreed that the kitchen looked much more furnished now there was something on the bare boards, and visitors – because, when you have a spare room it's amazing how people from outside just love to come up for a night or two – remark how wonderful it is to be young and strong, and of course a gift like writing is just ideal, because you can do it anywhere and in your own time.

Furnishing the 'workroom' called for careful thought. Eventually I bought a carpet, a 'rexine' set, the usual short chesterfield, and two large chairs, a straight chair for writing, a Tansad chair for typing, a pair of lace curtains, a pair of long brown silk ones, with a two-foot border of Egyptian figures and some window wedges. Aunt Kate gave me a clock and I put the picture of Mr Gilbert on the mantelpiece. Then I settled down to work.

During my seven years there I produced fourteen novels that were published, a good many short stories, some verses, and a play that was sent to Gerald du Maurier and consigned to the flames when he showed no interest in it. I was never more financially secure. Indeed, I had never known anything like it. In 1928 I could open a bank account with £300. Soon I had £200 in Savings Certificates and a running balance of three figures. I got American contracts, sold second rights, saw my work translated into half a dozen languages.

And, in spite of the Aberdeen terrier I bought for company during the first few months, I was lonelier than I had ever been in my life.

Chapter Eleven

During the first year, however, there was a diversion. The Vicar called with the incredible suggestion that one might care to join the ranks of the district visitors.

I was appalled. 'Of course not. I've never done such a thing in my life.'

'It's quite simple. You don't need to talk to them about their souls. Just be friendly.'

I looked at him, in distress. So that was what one looked like, after all one's care to select fetching and original get-ups from Pontings' Bargain Basement. One's winter coat now, only just acquired – a distinctive wine-colour, with a nutria collar and lined throughout, the whole costing three pounds – a black felt hat, bought in the Inexpensive Millinery, true, but worn at what an angle! – is it possible that the Vicar is so other-worldly that he has overlooked the chic of that ensemble? But most likely he got his great idea one wet morning when, from the security of his car, he saw his new parishioner bicycling round the shops in a voluminous mac and a beret.

After him came the Lady-in-Chief of the parish, for all the clergy were unmarried, and there were no wives to take charge of the numerous activities.

'It is a Great Compliment,' she assured me solemnly. 'The Vicar is Very Careful whom he chooses.'

'He's only spoken to me once before,' I murmured.

'The Vicar's judgement is Always Sound.'

She had brought little account books and notebooks and thrift cards and parish magazines and a list of addresses; she told me the District Visitors met in the Clergy House at II a.m. on first Wednesdays to pay in their money and get the Vicar's receipt; she said one's aim was to get more and more of the parish on to the thrift club, as that might be the thin end of the wedge. Eventually they might Come to Church. And if anyone was dying or sick or unbaptised I was to let the Vicar know.

The majority of my district regarded the Church as a kind of Poor Law Institution, without the embarrassment of making an application. They considered that, at the first sign of sickness or distress, the clergy should surge round with milk tickets and grants to holiday homes and new-laid eggs and chickens.

'The Vicar came and asked Mr S—— if he had a book to read, last time he was ill,' said Mrs S—— darkly. 'Not once did he ask: Have you enough to put in your stomach? That's not what we expect of the Church.'

When I reminded her there was a Relieving Officer round the corner, she folded her hands and said coldly, 'We're not come to that, I thank you, miss.'

Hardly any of them came to church. They said it was too high or else that the lady at the chapel had been so kind the last time they had trouble they didn't like to disoblige her. The Nonconformists told me frankly that the chapel didn't make these weekly collections, so they were glad enough to see me on Monday mornings, provided I came regularly, but when the Vicar called they wouldn't admit him further than the doorstep.

District Visiting is, on the whole, a maligned occupation. The Visitors themselves are the butt of music-hall artists and the men who supply comic pictures to the twopenny weeklies. Unfortunately, one has to admit that a lot of the pictures they produce are remarkably lifelike; there is supposed to be something 'worldly' about visiting in a Rose Valois model; or else D.V.s are cut from a special pattern and would not recognise a Rose Valois if they saw one. Anyway, whatever the reason, though they are undeniably faithful and the salt of the earth, they are seldom decorative.

'It isn't the business of salt to be decorative,' I was once told, when I made this rash criticism. 'It's only for flavouring purposes.'

Flavouring? I wonder. Still, no one I had met had ever suggested that District Visiting was fun. Not Good Works, not solemnly undertaken because you want to 'do your share' in the work of the Church, but plain unadulterated fun. Anyway, it was in that district in Ealing, the only fun I ever found in the place. The newcomer progressed through a number of stages. You began on the doorstep, fumbling with change and intricate entries in two different books, and two sets of cards. When the householder had made you realise that she was as good as you, if not better – some of them were much better; they went out in their children's cars on Sundays and did the weekend shopping on a scale that made your mouth water – then you were admitted to the 'parlour'. This was the best-furnished and least-used room of the house, and in the depths of winter it kept its spiral of coloured paper in the grate in place of a fire. My predecessor, I was told, had abandoned the work because she didn't care for this doctrine of equality. She wanted to be kind, but after all, she was an Honourable.

'I told her to her face,' said Mrs J——. 'Don't make the mistake of thinking that because we live in a small house we're of no account. If I worked before my marriage, it was because I chose to. It wasn't that I had to.'

When you were really 'accepted' by a family you went, by right, into the kitchen and heard how difficult husbands were, or how Herbert had married a girl who was no class really; and sometimes they would tell you their own life-histories. They enjoyed that, and so did I.

There was Mrs H——, a little sprig of a woman who

ruled her husband with a rod of steel. Her passion was for her son, Albert. She told me about his conception.

'When I first took Jim and we didn't have a family right away, like all my sisters, I didn't mind so much, because, being a nursemaid before marriage, I'd seen enough of kids. But after three years I noticed him watching other people's children in a funny sort of way, so I went to my doctor, and I said, "I've been married three years, doctor, and not so much as a miss in all that time. What can I do about it?" "Well, Mrs H——," said the doctor, "you must go on hoping." So I did, but that didn't get me far. Then one of my friends said: "Annie, why ever don't you get Jim to give you a bicycle?" "Give me a bicycle?" I said. "What on earth would I want with that?" "Well," she told me, "I have known it do the trick." So I asked Jim for a bicycle, though of course I didn't tell him why, because there's some things you can't talk about, not even to your husband. When I got it, I went out every day and I found Ellen was right. In no time I was carrying. Well, I went up to see my old mistress and I said to her, "Oh, Madam, I'm sure you'll be glad to know as I'm expecting," and she said, "Well, Annie, I am glad to hear that, because I know how you wanted a nursery." A bit before my time she sent for me again, and she took me into her drawing-room that was full of ladies; and you only had to give them one look to see what their trouble was. "Annie," she said, "I want you to meet these friends of mine. I told them about you and your bicycle, so they all got themselves bicycles, and look at 'em now."'

At first, too, I used to go to the District Visitors' meetings, partly because it was expected, and partly from curiosity. But this did not last long. District Visitors in the mass were a little too much for me. Plain and good they were, and their clothes were not even good. Before I joined their ranks, the Vicar, a ripe five-and-fifty, must have been the baby of the class. Contrary to my expectations this meeting did not open with prayer. The ladies beamed at the Vicar and he beamed back. They made little jokes with him and he made little jokes in return. One visitor, hurrying in at the tail of the procession, said anxiously, 'Oh, Vicar, I'm afraid I'm the last,' to which he replied – like a cue in amateur theatricals – 'Last but not least, Miss P—— last but not least.' So after a little I used to put my money through Miss M——'s letter-box, or waylay her in church and hand it to her, and get her to obtain the requisite receipt.

But even the District Visiting did not last long. At the end of the year things at home had become increasingly difficult. My mother was more ill, the charwoman more erratic. The district did not like being taken by surprise. The proper time for visiting was Monday mornings; and Monday morning was by no means the same thing as Tuesday afternoon. And if you missed a week, the majority spent the money they had intended to save. It wasn't right, they told you reproachfully, as though not merely you but the whole body of the Church Militant had betrayed them. After a little, I, too, felt it wasn't right, and one bitterly snowy day, when the charwoman had not been near us for three weeks and we had no substitute and no idea when, if ever, she would return, I told Miss M——, who had come to see what was happening, that I was afraid I must temporarily resign my district. I gave her back all the little books and the duplicate cards and the unsold parish magazines; I gave her my little bag with monies collected to date; I gave her the address of the woman whose little boy at nine years old had not been baptised; and she took them all in her brisk way and said she was sorry and the Vicar would be sorry, and she expected the District would be sorry and off she tramped down the path. She was one of the few people I have ever known who could ride through traffic in the rain with an open umbrella over her head, and put it down without dismounting.

After the gate had clanged behind her and there was nothing to be seen in the road but snow, inches deep, on the pavement, and more snow, hungry to fall, in the low grey skies, winter seemed to close completely round the house, a winter that lasted almost two years. I had never dreamed of such loneliness as this. During those two years scarcely any one opened the front gate, except Joan who came almost every Sunday night; the telephone was so silent that a wrong number was a welcome break in the monotony. The luncheon-visit of an occasional aunt was a red letter day. Life resolved itself into three departments – Illness, the House, Work.

Housework is an ungrateful expenditure of energy. Plates that have been washed after breakfast must be washed again after lunch; stairs that are swept on Monday must be swept again on Tuesday; beds, no matter how assiduously mattresses are turned and sheets tucked in, must be made every day, and in illness more often than that. The sideboard silver may take a whole afternoon to clean – silver kettle, twin tip-up bacon dishes, entrée dishes, biscuit-box, cheese dish, sauce tureen, egg-boiler (the same egg-boiler, with the same swan swimming serenely into space), the solid silver lamp that is only kept for ornament nowadays, the silver tray, the three silver teapots, the sugar-basins, cream-jugs, sweet dishes – but a couple of hours of fog and they are as yellow as brass and all's to do again.

> *Ten thousand times I've washed and dressed*
> *And all's to do again.*

as Housman very nearly said.

Elsewhere life rushed and crackled and roared; here the only difference in the days was whether the charwoman came or whether she didn't; if she didn't, it meant staying indoors until the evening, when my father returned. Sometimes, after dinner, sitting in the drawing-room, I would put aside my book and listen. Everything was deathly still; in a chair opposite my mother would be dozing; the dog slept on the carpet; in the study next door Father read. No sound anywhere. And if I slipped out of the big shadowy north room and opened the door leading to the garden, there was silence here, too, except for the shuffle of the wind in the trees. It was too quiet – it was unnatural. I would call the dog and we would go for a walk into the residential streets where the big houses stood. Here, on spring and summer evenings, the lights would be on and, often enough, the curtains remain undrawn. It is vulgar to look through other people's windows. But I was, presumably, vulgar, for I looked. I would see people gathered round tables, eating or playing cards or just talking; sometimes a door would open and a young couple would come hurrying down the drive, would leap into a car and vanish up west. I liked to stand by the gate where the bushes concealed me and hear those unknown voices. And in the side streets and on the Green were lovers. I liked to hear sharp voices calling through the silence, to hear the roar of cars, before we came back to find the house as still as when we left it. At ten o'clock the bedroom fire was lighted and hot-water bottles put in the bed; then I boiled a kettle for the final cup of tea that rounded off the day. The house was scarcely more quiet when it was asleep than it had been all day long.

When you know what loneliness is like you cease to laugh at the solitary women who make gods of their pets; you don't say, 'Oh, they're nuts,' when you see them coming along the streets, talking and smiling busily to themselves; you don't even agree, 'Of course they ought to be shut up,' when you find them writing letters to themselves or even posting boxes of violets to their own address in time for St Valentine's Day. They're not mad or even peculiar. They are desperately lonely people trying to keep sane.

Christopher came back on leave from the East in 1929, bringing with him his bride, a heavenly girl, so pretty it was a pleasure just to sit and look at her. They spent a few days with us at Christmas – my mother's health was so frail now that, although we could have housed a couple of newly-marrieds without being crowded, she could not have even such intimate guests as these for more than a few days. Their coming woke the house up; the telephone bell jangled, the postman came more often; they rushed about in a slick little blue two-seater. Everyone wrote to congratulate Mother on her charming daughter-in-law. They sat on the kitchen table – being Christmas we were, of course, without an Abigail – and ate slabs of bread-and-dripping. Even the dog became more lively. The day they sailed for Malaya my mother called me.

'You can get a doctor now,' she said. 'I think I am very ill.'

A few weeks later we shut up the house at Ealing and went into a flat at the seaside. It had always been my mother's ambition to spend her last days by the sea. Increasing pain and weakness must have clouded the pleasure she had always anticipated, but it was in a room looking right over the ocean that at last the end came.

When I saw her laid out for burial I thought I had never realised a human creature could look so small.

Chapter Twelve

That autumn, when I was still feeling about my new-found liberty as a puppy feels about a bone too large for it, not quite sure where to begin, Joan wrote from Stepney: 'Why not come and help here for a day or two each week? We want someone for the pensioners.'

In visualising London, the only London you are likely to experience, one pictures an area stretching from, say, Hammersmith Broadway to the Bank. But Stepney lies beyond all this.

The whole of the East End is honeycombed with streets of little houses, many of them so old and so unsafe that they have been condemned, in some cases for years. Yet they remain occupied on account of the difficulty of housing the tenants while the work of rebuilding goes on. Time and car fares are both important factors. A man who works in Poplar will not thank you for taking him away from his insanitary quarters in Pennyfields and putting him into clean rooms at Hackney. In these parts of London a man must live near his work. The Authorities are doing their best; everywhere the danger-spots are coming down, houses constructed inside of rotten wood, so that an overturned lamp would set the whole place ablaze, houses where you have to go round with a bit of soap catching fleas, houses where, in hot weather, the bugs come out of the wainscot. The Authorities are replacing these condemned dwellings with enormous blocks of flats. So far the East Ender has not taken kindly to this beehive type of existence; with all its disadvantages, he prefers the sort of house where he was born, although only a bit of it may be his. Only a bit! They live anywhere, these people – in basements, in attics, in rooms where you must have the light on all day. Some of the houses have to be seen to be believed. Water? There is a tap on the landing. Sanitation? An outside privy. Bathrooms? There are the public baths, where many women do their washing for the week. In big families the living-room becomes a sleeping apartment at night. They will agree that it oughtn't to be like that, if you put it to them, but they don't spend much of their time complaining. If they did they must, for numerically they are a vast army, have brought about some sort of revolution by this time. Or perhaps they prefer to expend their energies on other things. Anyhow, their philosophy is of the day-today variety. In a world where employment is precarious and a man can be stood off at a day's notice, it seems ridiculous to plan for improvements months ahead.

As for the new districts – Dagenham, for instance, where the Ford Motor Works are – many families who had good houses there came trickling back to rooms in Stepney, less because of the alleged damp – Dagenham is on the marshes – than because of the loneliness. They miss their neighbours, and householders will stay under the same roof for five-and-twenty years.

'There's lots of places worse than Stepney,' said an old woman to me last week. 'Anyhow, it is lively.'

Strangely enough, considering many of its adverse circumstances, that remains an accurate label. In work or out of it, Stepney is lively. And yet, it is well known as a great area for unemployment. Dressmaking, trouser-finishing, millinery, cracker-factory work, above all, casual dock labour – all these are seasonal jobs. In bad times – and 1930 was the beginning of that slump from which at present we have not recovered – it was common to find machinists and dressmaking hands who only had an average of two days' work a week. Beyond Stepney lie the Docks, and no man's living is more precarious than that of the casual dock labourer. It's desperately hard to get work and when you have got it you must work like a dog without even knowing whether you will be wanted tomorrow. The 'regulars' are not so badly off. They will tell you that, at rush times, the regular dock labourer, the man in permanent employment, will draw as much as eight pounds in one week. Many of the employers prefer to pay their own men overtime rates to employing casuals. There is always a certain amount of leakage in dock work, pilfering on the part of the employees, but a man in regular work is less likely to imperil his future. The casuals have a rough time of it. There are periods – the wool sales constitute one of them – when their hopes rise, for then practically any one can be sure of a few days' work; but in between you may get one or one and a half or even two days' employment in the week, and on the other days you must go down to the Labour Exchange and 'sign on' in order to draw your unemployment pay at the week's end. Then, you can never tell what the Government will do. It may decide to protect home trade by putting an enormous tariff on imported goods of some particular class; this is useful to the manufacturers of those goods and their workmen, but it increases unemployment at the Docks. If there is any trouble with the Dockers' Union, there is no hope of work until it has been settled. Dock labourers must be up very early and make their way to the dock where a ship is expected to unload; every casual must have a card – without it he has no chance of being taken on. On arrival each man does his best to attract attention from the foreman, for of the crowd at the gates only a proportion can be employed. If by some chance the dock has been changed, they must hustle along to the new one. Men who have been working at the docks for forty years complain that the modern bias is in favour of the younger men, and when you realise the muscular effort involved in much of this work you can scarcely be surprised. The unsuccessful must 'register' when they leave the Dock, in order to be eligible for 'unemployment' at the end of the week. Now and again it is thought worthwhile going down again at midday on the chance of more hands being needed.

During the war Ernest Bevin fought like a tiger-cat to get the men's daily wage raised to sixteen shillings, but now it is somewhere in the neighbourhood of eleven shillings. The cafés near the Docks open early, for in many families the wife cannot be up in time to give her husband breakfast before he goes out. Indeed, it is often the man who makes a pot of tea and brings her a cup before the day's work begins. For however the luck may go, the women are never out of a job.

The men who can accept 'relief', at the beginning anyhow, with equanimity are few. Now and again a man will tell you that he has paid rates all his life and is entitled to assistance when he is in deep water, but for the most part they will be driven to desperate straits before they apply for Poor Law Assistance. One of the reasons for this is that the law compels a man to make his own application; the wives would go more readily, for the children's sake, but the men hang back.

The introduction of machinery causes a temporary rise in the unemployment figures. A fish porter of thirty-six, who had been working in Billingsgate Market since he was fourteen, was told that an automatic machine had been installed that would do the work of three hundred men. This may easily mean permanent unemployment, for this man has no other trade, the unskilled labourer abounds for any work of that kind, and the Unions watch like eagles over their own members' interests.

This man had five young children and nothing to look forward to but a decline through Unemployment Benefit to Transitional Benefit, and finally to relief. In this part of London you will find any number of 'breadwinners' who have been unemployed for years, and never expect to work again.

The dislike of charity persists through every circumstance. Elderly women are sometimes practically carried to the Relief Office by the parish doctor, because what they are really suffering from is not indigestion or giddiness, but sheer starvation. In 1930 unmarried men seldom got relief in kind; unmarried women could get a money allowance for rent, and food tickets, but men would be offered the House, and from this they shrank. It didn't give them a chance for applying for jobs, they would tell you. But it goes deeper than that. The hatred of the House is universal, not because workhouses are not well run, but it spells the final concession to defeat, the acknowledgement that the game is up for good and all. The temptation to a young man to marry and thereby qualify for outdoor relief was considerable, and everywhere you find families all of whose children were born while the father was out of work. Large families are still the rule rather than the exception, though the time when it was considered pretty good to rear six children out of thirteen has passed.

Nowadays social services look after the delicate, and there are voluntary associations of every kind. 'It's the poor as 'elps the poor' still remains true. Landladies will allow the rent to run for weeks rather than eject a tenant. Sometimes the Society would be asked to pay back rent. It is only possible to do this when the man is likely to get back to work shortly, or when arrears are due to sickness. Otherwise, you are simply compensating the landlord, for if a family has no appreciable income, in a month's time they will be on the rocks again.

There exists a belief in the heart of practically every unemployed man that he has the ability to run a street stall. These abound in East London; go down Watney Street, Cayley Street, Burdett Road, Salmon Lane, everywhere you find the street market in full swing. Men offer five apples in the palm of the hand for twopence; tomatoes, oranges, bananas, are sold in the same way. Bunches of mint, lemons, children's drawers at threepence a pair, unnameable cuts of meat, smoked haddocks, old magazines, shoes at a shilling a pair, cheap silk stockings – there is little you cannot buy. In a class by themselves are Pussy's Butchers. Going the rounds, the inexperienced, lifting the knocker, may dislodge a small clammy parcel that, examined, proves to be twopennyworth of lights for the tenant's cat. Many cat owners have a regular order all the year round. In the Market in the Roman Road you can buy a second-hand saucepan or kettle for a penny or two, better, the old folks tell you, than the bright trash you get at the new cheap stores.

The pawnshop and the tallyman are two of the permanent features of East End life. The tallyman comes to your door with blankets, coats, suits, shoes. You pay him a shilling and the goods are yours. All you must do is to continue paying a shilling weekly for an indefinite period, sometimes after the shoes have worn out. In this way housewives often pay three or four times as much as they would give in shops, but the convenience of the system ensures its success. Allied to this is the Hire-Purchase System, often known as the Never-Never Way. Most of the hire-purchase furniture is appalling; quality poor, everything of the showiest, everything machine-made. Often a bait is offered a young couple setting up in one or two rooms by a 'gift' of a dreadful little machine-turned curb or an unframed mirror. These inexperienced people will contract for forty pounds' worth of furniture they could buy outright for less than half that sum. If payments fall too much behind, the hirers are entitled to collect the furniture, without any compensation – I speak of the law as it stood in 1930. The scandal of the system has caused drastic revision in legislation since then. The difficulty is to persuade the people to buy sound second-hand goods. They object to the principle.

The pawnshop in many households is as familiar as the milkman or the baker. It is a sure way of raising money for food in emergencies. However small the sum raised, you must pay interest; you pay a penny for your pawn-ticket, and a penny for a sheet of brown paper to wrap your goods when you redeem them. You can bring your own paper, if you like, but it is only the very brazen who will bring away their possessions unwrapped.

Experienced social workers ask about pawn-tickets at a first interview; experienced applicants bring them in their pockets. Lace curtains, boots, frocks, tablecloths, blankets, suits – curtains are left to the end, for when they are taken down from the windows the depths of your poverty is revealed to the whole street. The last thing to go is the wedding-ring. It is unlucky to pawn a wedding-ring, and if it must be done it is the first thing to be redeemed.

You will hear people say that the spirit of the poor has declined; young men nowadays throw up jobs for the most trivial reasons; they are satisfied to live on the 'dole'. This to some extent is true, but it is hard to blame the young. They do not look to the future, that promises little that is hopeful; they look back to the past and see the old people, who worked faithfully all their lives, pinched and saved, dependent on charity in their old age. The Old Age Pension of ten shillings is not enough, without other help, either from married children or, where this is not available, from the authorities or from some voluntary organisation. Most of them would prefer to see the Pension raised and the money being spent on A.R.P. shelters and the like saved to this end.

Case-fronts, on which applications are made, are as awe-inspiring as the forms one used to fill up at Employment Agencies. It is a ticklish job, particularly for the novice. No one likes asking for help, and information is often given in a truculent manner. The inexperienced worker is shy about asking so many questions – for how many there are! Name, age, birthplace, religion, occupation, doctor, details about the family, their school if they are still below earning age, their employers if they are not (though children's employers may not be approached except in unusual circumstances and then only with the child's consent), wages (or givings) of husband – many of these wives have no notion what their husbands earn – givings of children, pawn-tickets, sick-clubs, help from relief in the past, relatives, references, war service (if any). That is the first step. Follows the home visit, inspection of rent book, visits to relations and references, sometimes children to be seen, landlord to be interrogated, doctor's report obtained – no wonder it's a long job, and the same procedure must ensue when it's a matter of ten shillings as when it's a question of as many pounds. You cannot help a family because the wages earned are too low to meet expenses; this is simply supplementing, and encourages bad employers. Sometimes it seems impossible to make any constructive plan. At one time help would be given to set up a street stall, but without experience this scarcely ever keeps the applicants off the rates for as long as six months. A stall needs experience and flair; you never find established street traders coming for help. If they do strike a bad patch they contract private loans.

The deaf and dumb couple lived in a side street. The house was old, so old that inside it was pitch-dark. The staircase spiralled; you felt your way up by a rope stapled to the wall, that was greasy with the touch of thousands of hands. At the top of the stairs the deaf mute stood, holding out a candle to light you up. Behind him was his amazingly beautiful wife, making queer pleased noises like an animal. She was a superb creature, like a German Marguerite at thirty; golden hair, pink cheeks, blue eyes, dressed in a bright blue gown. Her husband was much older, very thin, unshaven, wearing black trousers, a dingy white shirt with neither tie nor neckcloth, a black waistcoat hanging open. The room was furnished like a kitchen. A kitchen table, a dresser, a big old-fashioned range, a surprising array of clean plates on the wall, no sign of food anywhere. They had sent an unintelligible letter to the Stepney office, from which it only appeared that they needed help. The impression it gave was one of imbecility. And indeed, the woman behaved like an idiot, throwing out her arms, clucking, gibbering, nodding her big smiling head, making indecipherable sounds. Neither they nor the visitor knew the deaf and dumb alphabet; nor did it seem as though they could read or write. They would take the paper on which a question was carefully printed in capitals, and shake their heads and gibber again. The man gesticulated fiercely, his face grim; the woman chuckled and looked across at her husband. Suddenly he leapt to his feet, went to the dresser and returned with a plate in either hand. He flung open the door of the oven, the door of the cupboard. All this presumably was to show that there was no food in the place. You wrote down the name of the Relieving Officer, but without result. Any sort of inquiry was futile. There was a daughter somewhere, but it was impossible to learn anything about her. The man shook his fist, the woman stretched her hands. They could not even produce a rent book. That might have shown if rent was due, and how long they had lodged here.

The woman on the ground floor scowled when questioned. 'I dunno anything about them. I keep meself to meself.'

'You must know how long they've been here.'

'Couldn't say, I'm sure.'

'Or whether they work.'

Her face darkened. 'I shouldn't worry.' She turned and went back to her kitchen. The hall was so dark you had to feel your way to the door.

What can Society do for people like these?

The old woman lived in a single room, dark with furniture and hoarded rubbish, in Shadwell. The furniture was so large and there was so much of it that it was difficult to cross the room. She herself informed you she was eighty, so far as she knew, and had been here for more than twenty years. She complained of her landlord; he pestered her, she said, always wanting to repaper the room. But she couldn't have her 'things' knocked about by a lot of workmen. The walls were ingrained with dirt, the floor indescribable. She herself was a little dwarf of a creature, with a face so dark it was hard to see where the shabby brown jersey began and her thin brown neck ended. There appeared to be no washing facilities in the room, but there was a tap at the end of the passage. The usual scrap of margarine in a saucer, the heel of a loaf and an open tin of condensed milk stood on the table. The usual pot of stewed tea simmered on the hob. Did she ever eat anything else? One never learned. And why do these old women always buy condensed milk? Well, it's cheaper for one thing, and it's ready sweetened; but what they really mean is that it's what they grew up on and they detest change.

On the chairs were piles of old, old rags – her clothes, she said. She was mending them. On the walls – photographs, on the mantelpiece – ornaments that didn't know what a duster looked like. At the windows hung curtains stiff with grime; the scrap of lace curtain hanging between them was the only comparatively clean thing in the room.

'It's the coalman,' she said vindictively. 'Landlord give me a cupboard for me coal. I don't like coal in a living-room, never did, but I've nowhere else to keep it.'

She swept some rags off a chair. 'Sit down and make yourself comfortable. All these noo-fangled ideas. Don't hold with them. These parts ain't what they was. No life these days.'

There must have been life and to spare in those filthy wainscots, probably more life in the rags that have just been pushed off the chair where you are yourself sitting.

'When I was a girl now, times was lively then. I've seen women stripped to the waist fighting with knives in the Ratcliff Highway. They don't do that no more.'

She sighed heavily for the days that were gone.

'I've known times when the police couldn't go down

some of these alleys, except in twos, and when it wasn't uncommon to find a body slung in the gutter outside the public house of a morning.'

These were usually the bodies of sailors, strange men of every colour, who had been decoyed thither from the docks, made drunk, robbed of their money, and stabbed if they made trouble. If a policeman inquired too closely, became 'nosey', particularly if he looked like tracing the murder home to any particular individual, as like as not his body would be found in a gutter, too.

'Pennyfields!' brooded the old woman. 'Look at it now. All the shop windows with Chinese names on top and 'Cups of Tea tuppence' underneath. It wasn't tea and tinned pineapple they sold when I was a girl. Why, the lords and ladies used to come down to these parts to see a bit of life in those days. It wasn't safe to go those ways after dark. Now you could go any time, and you wouldn't see nothing.' Montmartre, her tone suggested, the Montmartre of the Apache and the melodramatic play, had nothing on the East London of sixty years ago.

Nothing of that remains now, she says bitterly, except the old houses crumbling into decay. 'And flats. Living like mice in holes. And interference all the time ...'

Education? What use is education? Where does book-learning get you, or being able to write your name? There are plenty of the old ones who can't do either. They started their earning lives at eight or nine years old, getting a shilling a week and their food, minding the neighbour's youngest while the new baby was being born. They scrubbed tall shelves, climbing on to chairs to reach them, bought their food in pennyworths. Nobody helped you in those days; there were no pensions for the old, no aid for widows. If you lost your man you took in washing and brought your children up without being indebted to anyone. A neighbour lent a hand over child-birth, and if some of the infants died, well, it was God's Will. No one blasphemed in those days or questioned the dictates of Providence. Funerals were greater occasions than births, especially if there was insurance money to be drawn. Once the burying was over, the rest of the day was given up to celebration. From pub to pub you went, standing rounds of drinks until the money was exhausted. Sometimes you ended up in quod, for D. and D. But all that was over now. Look at the present method of conducting funerals, hole-in-a-corner, as if you were ashamed of them, no skylarking, nothing. Oh, times have changed indeed. It wasn't necessary to read then to get a bit of life; it flared up all round you. Even as late as 1911 there had been the Battle of Sydney Street, with huge crowds gathered round the besieged house, despite the volley of bullets, and at the last the whole place going up in flames.

What a hold on life they had, those old women. With a vocabulary of certainly no more than six hundred words, with an expression, an occasional gesture, they could reconstruct for you a whole phase of life that had already gone past. The rich dark mysterious life, packed with incident, of a people as alien in blood and temperament as Russians or Japanese, living in the heart of an English community, speaking their own tongue, keeping their own counsel. A people of the most tremendous vitality, so that the whole city seethed with life. What an opportunity they offered to the novelist!

Chapter Thirteen

Variety is the spice of life. After Stepney the Hiawatha.

One evening my telephone rang. A strange voice said: 'I don't suppose you remember me, but my name is ___ ___.'

I remembered her at once; she was, indeed, a woman difficult to forget.

'I have been thinking of you for some time. I think you should get about more. Now, what about joining a Club?'

I was staggered. I didn't know a single person who belonged to a Club, except a bridge or croquet club, and she could hardly mean those.

'You would meet some Very Nice People that way,' the voice went on.

'Oh, yes,' I said. Nothing more.

'I'm not sure yet which would be the best for you. You don't want to do anything in a hurry, and it's important to find the Right One. But I want you to know I am Keeping My Eyes Open. I will ring up again later.'

Then, for several weeks, nothing happened. I thought – I did not know her very well in those days – that she had forgotten me. Then the telephone rang again.

'Are you free on Tuesday night?'

'I am. Yes, of course.' Of course I would be.

'I have two tickets for a party at the Hiawatha. I think that would be a Very Good Club for you.'

A party! Snakes! 'Does that mean evening dress?'

'Certainly. Meet me at Notting Hill Gate Underground Station at seven-fifteen.'

I had not owned or needed an evening dress since 1927. I went to Bourne & Hollingsworth and bought an apple-green georgette with a Victorian posy on the bosom. At seven-fifteen on Tuesday evening I was waiting in a slight mist at the appointed rendezvous. Some accident delayed her; I half made up my mind that this was the wrong night and it would be best to return to Ealing. For what had Women's Clubs to say to me? I knew only too well I had nothing to say to them. However, while I hesitated, an imposing figure loomed up, and we were off.

My first glance of the hall of the Hiawatha was illuminating. I perceived that this was no mere Club – it was a movement. A movement in the education of women. There literally wasn't a single interest for which some group or section did not cater. If I were a member I should have the choice of attending a lecture by a prominent airwoman, a lunch to be given to a well known journalist, a dinner to an eminent foreign novelist and

some scarcely less eminent English ditto, a debate on
– I cannot recall after so many years – an expedition
with the Geographical Section, a visit to the BBC, a
lecture on 'The Beginnings of Life' by a naturalist, or a
cocktail party at which a number of celebrated actors
and actresses would be present. (At that date I had never
been to a cocktail party and had an instinctive awe of any
one who had.) If I didn't want to be educated, thrilled or
entertained, I could play bridge, ping-pong, or billiards,
or have my hair waved on the premises.

At this stage my companion scooped me up, saying,
'This isn't the party, you know.' I followed her meekly. As
we disappeared two women met in the hall opposite the
notice about the Beginnings of Life lecture.

'That might be interesting, do you think?'

'One-and-six. And it'll only be flowers.'

Upstairs, the handsome room was simply packed with
women, all, of course, in evening dress, and some in very
evening dress, if you know what I mean. The buzz of
conversation was like the buzz of Mr Wells's giant wasps.
I was frankly terrified. If there had been a sofa I would
have got under it. But there wasn't. Only a little bench
and some chairs, the small gilt kind where even a kitten
couldn't have found sanctuary. I'd never seen so many
women together in my life before.

Once, when I was quite young, my mother took me
to the Zoological Gardens. By one of the main gates was
an enclosure full of very handsome horned cattle, the
kind with humped shoulders, very like the coats women

are wearing at this moment. A label hung on the bars. These Animals Are Dangerous.

On the way back, she said, 'And which of the animals did you like best?'

I had to think. Then, 'Well, I thought the Dangerous were rather nice,' rhyming the word to go with Kangaroos, 'but, of course, I'm glad they were all in cages.'

Well, that first night at the Hiawatha I thought I had got into the Dangerous' enclosure, with all the bars down.

It was an excellent entertainment. There was an immensely fat man who played the piano with his behind, and after him a Russian (or perhaps she was a Latvian or a Pole) who held your handkerchief a moment and then told you your character. That went on for a long time. When the entertainers had been swept away for refreshments, the party forgathered. I forgathered by myself in the corner of my bench. I looked for my companion, but she was some distance off, simply surrounded. I couldn't attempt to join her. After a few minutes I was startled to hear myself addressed.

'I hear you are going to join the Club,' said a voice. 'You are a writer?'

'Well, I've had a few books published,' I acknowledged.

'I wrote books when I was younger,' said the lady. She then told me her name. I had never heard of it.

Then she said that she was one of the representatives of the Authors' Board, a very strong section but, naturally, needing fresh blood. I could see that she intended to have mine.

'Have you had your form yet?'

You can't do anything in this country, from the hour of your birth, without a form. Even after you're dead, somebody fills in forms for you. I said: No, I hadn't had a form yet; I hadn't asked for one, so she said she would introduce me to the Club Secretary. The Club Secretary said: I suppose you know two members who will propose and second you, and I said: Well, I know ———, mentioning the name of my hostess, but to my dismay the Secretary said: She is not a member of this Club.

However, it appeared that this did not necessarily mean I couldn't become a Hiawathan; I must produce three acceptable social references. Instantly I played my trump card – the Bishop. But there had been a war, times were changing, Bishops were no longer what they had been. It appeared that the Bishop was No Use. My references must all be women. Again I suggested my hostess.

'Yes. And two others. They should be magistrates or doctors or J.P.s. Don't you know any one like that?'

I looked at her humbly. 'No, I'm afraid I don't. The women I know are all pure, home-loving people who don't seek the limelight. Hasn't the Hiawatha any use for them?'

It appeared that the Hiawatha had not. That seemed to rule me definitely out. After all, I'd done my best, but if it was written in my stars that I could never be that mysterious and terrifying creature, A Clubwoman, well, there was nothing more to be done about it. I hoped

———— wouldn't feel I had accompanied her on false pretences.

However, presently we went downstairs to a cold collation of lemonade and chocolate eclairs, and while I was snouting round for something more solid I felt a touch on my arm. I turned. There stood L——, a charming friend of Joan's, whom I had met once or twice.

She said, 'I didn't know you were a member,' and I said, 'Well, actually, they won't have me, because I don't know the right people.'

She said, 'Oh, nonsense, you know me. What more do they want?' Then she tapped the arm of Some One Very Important Indeed, and said, 'You'll second her, if I put her up, won't you?'

The Very Important Person, whom I had once met for about two minutes at a social services tea-party, said, 'I'll put her up and you can second her. Don't give another thought to it,' she added to me. 'It will be Quite All Right.'

And so it was. I filled in my form and a little later I was notified that I was a member of the Hiawatha Club for Women. I was excited at having been found worthy, but I knew I should never, never have the courage to enter that Club alone.

But, in case the miracle happened, I got a little book on cocktails and learned the names, because at that time I found it difficult not to confuse them with the sundaes I occasionally bought at Lyons' Corner House.

Women join clubs for every kind of reason. One of

them, and perhaps the best, is a desire to Meet Some Nice People. But there are others. In a Club you can escape from your home, you can feed people whom you don't want in your flat, you can rest and have a nice cupper tea after shopping, you can get drinks a few minutes earlier and a few minutes later than you can in the local public house, you can get a bath if your own hot-water supply fails, and you can, if not actually hobnob with the great, buy a ticket for a dinner or a lecture and watch them from afar. I contented myself with this last for my first year. Naturally, as a very new member, I only sat in out-of-the-way corners, and caught glimpses of three-quarter profiles; but as time went on I crept up the scale until now I am sometimes put at the High Table itself. Besides these grand affairs, when men of mark came to dine and afterwards to speak, there were the domestic evenings, when members could do the talking. We could join issue over the infamy of publishers, agents and practically every other living author. I picked up some useful phrases.

'It's a bit tragic, really, to put your whole soul into a book and find that nobody else cares.'

'I always say that we authors don't write with ink, but with our heart's blood.'

Famous authors become Vice-Presidents; not so famous authors sit on Committees. Presently I, too, sat on a Committee. I must, during my first year, have been the ideal member. I turned up at every meeting and never opened my mouth except to say, 'What a good idea!' That was six years ago, and they still re-elect me every year.

But, of course, to me the Hiawatha really means the Bar. When I was first a member the bar was called the Buttery in olde englyshe letters on a background of olde englyshe hand-painted leaves; it was full of little glass-topped tables, with tub chairs to match; there were a lot of writing-tables sprinkled about, and if you wanted an alcoholic drink you put your head through a little black hole and whispered something, and presently a hand came out holding a small glass, and you took it and went to sit at one of the glass-topped tables. But suddenly all that was changed. The tables vanished and so did the hand-painted leaves. A long counter appeared, with stools, and seats round the walls, and glass tables and chromium chairs, and nowadays it often isn't easy to get a seat there after opening-time. The level of conversation has risen too. Only the other day I was told by a lady that I ought to practise thrift; thrift was one of the basic facts of nature. Even the caterpillar stored up honey for its young.

It is my belief that women who jeer at Women's Clubs are those who, for some reason, are not eligible for membership. If they don't believe me, let them join the Hiawatha and see the world.

By this time a thing called The Slump was beginning to set most of us by the ears. Books were affected, like everything else. Not only did our sales cease to increase according to expectation, but our American markets began to fail, until for a good many of us they no longer existed. America, we were told, is not interested in the contemporary English novel. The truth was that America has always been interested in one aspect of the English novel, and those authors who were fortunate enough to have gained a foothold in the affections of that public were secure enough. But those whose footing had always been precarious were finding themselves being edged out of the field.

My books, with one exception, had never achieved much popularity in the States, although for several years now they had been accepted and quite respectable advances paid. But after I learned that when my contract came to an end the publishers did not feel inclined to renew it, I began to get panicky and cast round for some fresh way of bringing the necessary grist to the mill. I called on my agent.

I said, 'What is your recipe for a sure-fire bestseller?'

He said, without an instant's hesitation, 'Young Love. You can't go wrong.'

I thought I could go extremely wrong. I had no experience of young love, and the love that you learn after thirty is quite a different kind, and certainly not suitable for bestsellers. Anyway, love stories must have a conventionally happy ending.

That avenue being closed, my best chance seemed to lie in the direction of the thriller. To the uninitiated all detective stories are thrillers; he does not recognise any distinction. But actually all that a thriller need do is thrill. You need not pay much attention to psychology, probability, King's English or logic; what you must do is construct a swiftly moving story, in which the incidents are pegged out like washing hung on a line. The line connects them, but they have little relation to one another. You need waste no time on subtleties; there are no rules to follow; you can make use of gangs, dope, mysterious Chinamen, intuition, coincidence and mumbo-jumbo, all those elements I was later to agree to forswear. But that time had not yet come.

I had no illusions. A thriller, written by me, would be written simply for the money it might bring in. I chose the usual house-party, with a particularly venomous old father done to death by one of his own family. I assembled the clichés and hoary properties I had hitherto disdained – secret passages, doors mysteriously opening, panels in the wall, anonymous letters, abductions, stolen gems, racing motors, villains disguised as the police, concealed writing, vamps and Chinamen. I mapped out the first chapter. It was pretty dreadful, but it certainly did thrill. I allowed myself three weeks to complete the book. After that I need never look at the thing again. I could even get someone else to proof it.

During the first week there came to the local cinema a film starring a man whose work I admired beyond words. To me, he was the artist *par excellence*. I never missed any picture in which he appeared. I had made such strides in the thriller that I determined to give myself an afternoon off. I paid my shilling and was admitted to a huge, empty dress circle, upholstered in sapphire-coloured plush. I settled down to two hours of reverential bliss.

That was one of the worst afternoons I had known for years. Within five minutes of the lowering of the lights I knew something was wrong. Dreadfully wrong. This man, whom I had placed little lower than the angels, had allowed himself to be starred (presumably for financial reasons) in a third-rate film that must have made any of his admirers wince. The thing went from bad to worse. We were shown Affliction overwhelming the Hero; his instant capitulation, his petulant decision to fight no more. For a brief moment he stood poised over eternity on a window-sill; but before he could take the leap that would have brought the performance to a welcome close, the door was pushed open and (you have guessed, of course) his faithful manservant, clad all in black, entered with an open Bible in his hand.

'Are not two sparrows sold for one farthing and are not ye much better than they?'

The obvious retort was, 'Kindly return to your own business in the pantry, Bunter, and leave me to mine,' but instead of even this amount of spirit, the Hero climbed meekly down from the sill and spent the rest of the picture in Doing Good on an ostentatious scale. I have forgotten the end of the film, perhaps I did not stay to witness it – but I do remember rushing out into the sunshine, swearing never again to go to a picture featuring this particular star. It seemed to me abominable that for mere money – and there I was brought up short. For it became clear to me that the difference between us was one of degree only. Sobered, I returned home, tore my thriller to shreds, flung the pieces into the basket, and settled down to decide how this story would have been if Dostoevsky had written it.

It wasn't finished in three weeks; it was written and rewritten; when at length it left my hands, a manuscript signed with the name of Anne Meredith for the first time, it was more months before it found a publisher. When it appeared some time in 1933 its reception, though mixed, was vastly entertaining. E. M. Delafield, in the *Morning Post*, considered that the author might one day write a good detective story or, less probably, a good psychological novel, but this one fell between two stools. The *New Statesman* said it was a masterpiece of psychological detective fiction. Sylva Norman, in the *Spectator*, hoped the author would never be tempted to write a real detective story in which her fine judgement and distinction of thought and style would inevitably be murdered. Ellis Roberts detested it, saying he didn't care who was murdered or by whom. Dorothy Sayers praised it; so did the anonymous critic of the *Observer*. More encouraging still was the cable from an American publisher who wanted to buy it, and my return cable accepting his offer. The American edition had one of those unforgettable covers that are among the things the Americans do better than ourselves. One critic even mentioned Dostoevsky.

It was clear that the effects of the slump were unlikely to be permanently offset by books modelled, be it ever so faintly, on the works of Russian genius, but on the whole it was as well that I had decided not to proceed with my original idea of writing thrillers, for, before *Portrait of a Murderer* was published, I had received an invitation to become a member of the Detection Club.

The letter of invitation was signed by Dorothy Sayers, who explained at some length the aims and objects of the Club. I didn't mind what its objects were. Everything snobbish in my system acclaimed this opportunity to hobnob with the Great. And the Detection Club is very snobbish indeed. It was founded some years ago by Anthony Berkeley, to be an association of the aristocracy of the detective-writing world. Conditions of admission were exceedingly rigid; popularity had nothing to do with it, sales had nothing to do with it. In no circum-stances could a thriller-writer be admitted. If Edgar Wallace and Sydney Horler had come to the gates with their hands full of gold they would have been turned away. I hold no particular brief for the aristocracy, but it is pleasant to be counted, once in a while, among their number.

My invitation was signed by Dorothy Sayers. The first time I saw that name in print was during the last year of the war, when I read a notice, in the *Poetry Review*, of a volume of verse, a slender volume of verse called *Op. I*, by a new writer obviously fresh from College. Dorothy Sayers was her name. Since then she had made her reputation in other fields, yet it was always as the young poet that I thought of her. She would, I thought, be slender and aloof – willowy, I think, was the word I had in mind. I saw the list of members. E. C. Bentley, G. K. Chesterton, Agatha Christie, H. C. Bailey, F. Wills Crofts, J. J. Connington, John Rhode ... I wanted not so much to meet Mr Rhode as to see him. He was published by my publishers, but if we contrived to appear during the same month, he was always above me on the list. I pictured him one of these young dark sardonic men, with a black lock falling over his nose. Infinitely superior. Quite typical of him to be elected to the Club before any one suggested my name, I thought.

The great day arrived. I put on the green georgette and, nervous at the thought of the exalted company I was to meet, came, not too early, to the Northumberland Avenue hotel where the dinner was to take place. A massive and majestic lady in (I think) a black dress swam towards me.

'I am Dorothy Sayers,' she said.

After that I'm not in the least surprised that I failed to recognise my first publisher – the first of my acquaintance, I mean – Mr Sadleir, looking like all the private detectives of one's dreams. One thing, he didn't know me either.

Mr Chesterton was the Club's first President. That first dinner I attended was his last. The 'Uncommon Order of Initiation' was worthy of the Club. Dinner (at which the menu was expressed in terms of blood) being ended, the members not concerned in the ceremony and all the guests were shooed into another room, while the procession formed up. It set forth in this order:

Two Torchbearers
Eric the Skull (the Club's mascot) borne on a Black
    Cushion by John Rhode
The Secretary (Dorothy Sayers)
The Candidates (Anthony Gilbert and E. R.
    Punshon)
The Sponsors bearing Torches (Margaret Cole and
    Anthony Berkeley)
The President (G. K. Chesterton)

Mr Chesterton can seldom have been more magnificent than he was in this role. A gigantic figure in a black gown, he turned majestically in the hall that was lighted only by the torches aforesaid, and the rest of the procession moulded itself before him. On either side stood the Torchbearers; behind them Mr Rhode with Eric. On either side the sponsors, between these the trembling candidates (at least, I speak for myself; I don't think Mr Punshon felt a qualm). Mr Chesterton, in a voice that might have come from the abyss, put the questions; Miss Sayers, in a voice that might have made the angels tremble, made the responses. My sponsor whispered fiercely, 'Hang your head a little, can't you? You are only a neophyte.'

It was a glorious experience; I felt as though I were marching to my wedding in the condemned cell. My bright frock supplied the only touch of colour about the proceedings. Afterwards, I was informed that black was the correct wear – to complete the condemned cell impression, I suppose. But the green frock was still the only one I had.

The Ceremony proper began by the President inquiring in the voice aforesaid:

What mean these Lights, these Ceremonies and this Reminder of our Mortality? (That was a dig at Eric.) In reply to which the Secretary indicated the two candidates.

These, having been sponsored and seconded, and having expressed their desire for admission, the President continued: Do you promise that your detectives shall well and truly detect the crimes presented to them, using those wits which it may please you to bestow upon them and not placing reliance upon nor making use of Divine Revelation, Feminine Intuition, Mumbo-Jumbo, Jiggery-Pokery, Coincidence, or the Act of God?

If Miss Sayers's voice made the angels tremble, mine must have made the devils beware. Like the Lost Chord, I have never been able to find it again.

I do.

Do you solemnly swear never to conceal a Vital Clue from the Reader?

I do.

Do you promise to observe a seemly moderation in

the use of Gangs, Conspiracies, Death Rays, Ghosts, Hypnotism, Trapdoors, Chinamen, Super-Criminals, and Lunatics, and utterly and forever to forswear Mysterious Poisons unknown to Science?

I do.

Will you honour the King's English?

I will.

The Candidate – did I mention that as the procession approached the room had been plunged into darkness, except for the light of the torches? – then took the Oath, one hand placed trustingly on Eric the Skull.

All this I solemnly do swear. And I do furthermore promise and undertake to be loyal to the Club, neither purloining nor disclosing any Plot or Secret communicated to me before publication by any fellow-members, whether under the Influence of Drink or otherwise.

Mr Punshon having taken a similar oath we were both acclaimed Members of the Club, and Mr Chesterton received us as under.

N. and M., you are duly elected members of the Detection Club, and if you fail to keep your promises, may other writers anticipate your plots, may your Publishers do you down in your contracts, may Total Strangers sue you for Libel, may your pages swarm with misprints and your Sales continually Diminish.

After that all the members said 'Amen' and the torches went out. As soon as the lights came on in the room, there was a rush for the bar, which had thoughtfully been erected at one end.

Mr Rhode came over to say, 'I'm very glad you are one of us now.' He was considerably older than I was and weighed seventeen stone.

Chapter Fourteen

Unexpectedly I achieved an American publisher for my detective novels and, equally unexpectedly, I was invited to a cocktail party given by his representative at the Gargoyle. This was my first literary cocktail party, and I didn't know what to wear. On the day itself I took down my winter coat and examined it anxiously. Nobody, I argued, was likely to pay any attention to me, really my clothes were not of importance; the coat, well-brushed, would not look too bad. It was black and black was always 'smart'. And if it had stretched a little when it was cleaned, probably my girth had spread a little since I bought it. The fur collar, well-brushed, would still look glossy under the electric light. I regarded the remark of a well-wisher, that it was about time that fur went back to the rat it came from, as poor taste. However – walking the dog round the town that morning I had seen, in Ealing's most exclusive dress shop, a perfect cocktail suit. It was made of black corduroy velvet, with a squirrel tie. With it, I could wear my new black felt, one of those bang-over-the-eye hats that were being worn that season. I hung up the coat and settled down to work. But it was no good.

I lifted the telephone receiver. 'Will you put me through to your costume department? You have a black velvet suit in your side window? Could you tell me the price?'

The unknown voice told me.

I said with commendable self-control, 'Thank you. I expect to get two suits for that,' and went back to work.

At five minutes to one I walked into that shop and said, 'Will you show me the black velvet suit you have in your side window?'

It was a safe enough move. The suit would not fit. Ready-mades do not take kindly to my figure; if they are big enough on the shoulders they are too big somewhere else.

This suit might have been built for me. Madame said so, and although I seldom agree with Madame, this time I had no choice. I could find no fault at all; I wrote out a cheque and carried the suit home.

I had been told that it was correct to arrive rather late for a cocktail party. It was so wet that I hesitated about risking the velvet suit at all. What with one thing and another it was even later than I had intended when eventually I did arrive, and there were not more than eight or ten people left. Someone greeted me and asked my name. When she heard it she said: Oh, then you must meet David. David wore an inconspicuous blue suit and an inconspicuous amount of dark hair.

As soon as we were introduced, he exclaimed, 'Are you an author?'

'Yes,' said I, who had assumed that no one else would be admitted to a literary cocktail party.

He seemed anything but pleased. 'I thought I was the only writer here,' he said pettishly. 'Lally,' he attracted the attention of a woman in green who appeared to be the hostess, 'there's another writer here.'

Lally, without looking over her shoulder, said comfortingly, 'Well, darling, I don't suppose any one's ever heard of him.'

'I have,' said David, disgruntled.

Lally turned and saw me. She said, 'How wonderful of you to come,' and told a waiter to bring me a drink. Somebody else brought me a cigarette. The woman who had first greeted me began to point out the other guests. That woman worked in a publishing house; that man over there told Mr Howard Spring what to recommend for the *Evening Standard* Book of the Month. Another round of drinks was offered; gradually we coalesced. I was introduced to Mr Spring's C.A. (confidential adviser). He looked at me in gratifying surprise.

'That's very interesting,' he said. 'I always thought Anthony Gilbert was a politician.' Then he took another drink – the drinks at this party went round like Catherine wheels – sat on the table and observed in cosy tones, 'Now let's tell each other about our operations.'

'Oh no,' said the middle-aged woman in black beside me, 'I couldn't.' It appeared that she had recently had a major operation of an extremely delicate nature.

'I've only had tonsils out,' said the young man who had brought me a cigarette, 'and that's such a dull scar to show.'

'Well, darling,' said Lally, 'we weren't thinking of showing our scars.'

'When I had appendicitis,' began my mentor …

'Appendicitis doesn't count,' ruled the C.A.

'Not even a split scar?'

'You're sure it was a split scar?' demanded David (I don't know his other name) in suspicious tones. 'Not just a swab in the wound? That wouldn't count. That happens to nearly everyone.'

'No, a real split scar. It was when I jumped off the top board at the school baths …'

'Nothing that happens at school counts,' announced the C.A. sweepingly.

Then we got down to it. I said nothing, for I had never had anything more serious done to me than a splinter taken out of my finger with an unsterilised needle, but I hoped, if I kept silence, they would suppose I had had appendicitis at least. The fun was fast and furious.

It was capped by the C.A., who said, 'After I had had appendicitis – no, I know that doesn't count – I was still Far From Well. So I went back to my doctor and he diagnosed a duodenal ulcer.'

'So you had another operation,' suggested Lally, hope-fully.

'Nothing of the kind. I had Mr Maclean's powder, and I was kept on a diet of a pint of milk and one egg a day for nine months.'

Another round of drinks appeared. I had stopped short at the second, and smoked cigarettes instead.

'Nine months?' said Lally, dreamily. 'Isn't that rather a significant period?'

I came away soon after that. I don't suppose one of them had noticed my velvet suit.

It would be cowardly to attempt a book on author-ship without tackling that most difficult of all questions, where does the author find his characters? It is the first question you are asked, if you've only published a couple of books. A good many people, of course, recognise themselves or their friends in everything you write. Or else they don't recognise themselves but they recognise someone else; either way their pride is hurt. They say, 'So you really think I'm like that!' or 'I suppose you don't think I'm an interesting person at all. Of course, if you really *knew* me!' And indeed there are a few authors – I believe Somerset Maugham is one – who will tell you that all their principal characters are drawn from life. But it is a common experience to authors to be told, if they attempt to do anything of this kind, that the one unreal character in the book is the character you took from among your acquaintance. It isn't hard to understand why. We are all of us so many people, and automatically we display different personalities according to the company in which we find ourselves. So that the person whom A knows might be practically unrecognisable by B.

There is – or was – a quite common police observation test that consisted of sending a number of men on to a stage, each performing a different action, while an audience watched them for a stated period. Then the curtain fell and the spectators were asked to write down what they had seen. It always happened that no two accounts were ever alike, and sometimes were so dissimilar that it was difficult to realise that two onlookers were describing an identical scene. One man's attention would have been so completely held by a particular performer that the rest of the show practically speaking passed him by. One would be attracted by the appearance of the players, another by their actions. And that is a rough example of how we, as individuals, strike our little world.

Obviously, then, few, if any, of us know any other person sufficiently well to portray him in a novel; the fact is, we are too personal in our relationships to be able to describe our friends impersonally. And it is the impersonal attitude of the author towards his characters that gives him his knowledge of them. You may hear an author say, 'I positively fell in love with A or B while I was writing about him (or her).' But the point to note is that this happened after the writing began. X did not start a book with any violent predilection in favour of any particular character. One might be noble, another foul, but he was not their judge, he was their recorder.

People who do not write books have very vague ideas as to how it is done. They say: How lovely to be inspired, to feel you must put a story on to paper. Very few novelists are inspired and I have never met one who did not dislike the actual work of transcription. Nor do characters – main characters certainly – spring to life in the mind, like Athene springing from the head of Zeus. The conception of a book is a much more tentative affair than that. We will assume that you have in mind the sort of book in which the plot is subservient to the character. Most great novels are of this kind; because it is folly to imagine, as some people do, that a man who is successful, or a man to whom much has happened is necessarily interesting. A man may be immensely successful, in the sense that he 'does well for himself', makes money, gets on, and yet be as dull as the proverbial ditchwater. It is people and not the things that happen to them who are interesting.

Assuming, then, that you have the urge to write and want to write about somebody rather than something, it is highly unlikely that you will wake up one morning with your central character clearly etched on your mind. The odds are that you will undergo weeks – occasionally it is months – of a profound unease. Someone who ought to know once described it to me as being in birth-throes. Something is going to happen, but you can't be sure when. For myself, this period is always one of great depression. When I am not writing I am not more than half-alive. I am miserable, hopeful, and dejected by turns. Then slowly someone emerges out of all this mental fog. He is not clearly seen at once, but like a form glimpsed through trees; presently some obstacle may conceal him; then he is visible again; he begins to take on personality. He grows in one's mind, does not leap into it. And even when your character has been perceived, you have still to learn his story. You cannot be arbitrary about this. Too many writers say: I have a good working knowledge of a certain phase of life and this man shall be pressed into that frame. Unless that is the right frame for him, your story cannot ring true. Anybody who has ever tried to write knows this.

St John Ervine, in an article in the *Observer* some years ago, wrote:

My belief is that he [the author] ought to be so intimate with them [his characters] that he can tell you trivial facts about their lives before they appeared in his pages. Characters do not come alive on page one of a book, nor do they cease to live on the last page, unless, of course, they are killed in the course of the story. The reader ought to have a sense of continuity about them. He ought to feel, in opening their book, he is opening a window in the wall of the house in which they live, that there is a great deal more of their life in that house than he can see through the window ... I once told Mr Bernard Shaw that I knew so much about the characters in my own play, *John Ferguson*, that I could tell him what crops were growing in the fields outside Ferguson's farm ... I believe that the people in my plays have an existence apart from me, that, in fact, they are there all the time, waiting for me to lift a curtain or open a window to look at them. When I write a play or a novel, I am telling a story that would still be a fact if the story were not told at all. Any claim to recognition that I have lies in my ability to tell what I see with enough veracity and skill to make it interesting to those who have not seen it. I have not created my people; I have revealed them. They are not my servile creatures; they exist by themselves.

From the same paper I took a cutting, expressing similar views, from another novelist:

> These are no shadows conjured in the mind,
> Their radiant beauty from no fancy blown,
> These are bright buds on an immortal stem.
> Souls that see clearly where my eyes are blind,
> Who know swift ardours I have never known,
> And I am but the glass that mirrors them.

And there is a line in Clemence Dane's *Legend* that sticks in my memory:

She knows – she proves that she knows – things she can't possibly know.

(This, actually, is less irrelevant than it appears.)

By 1933 the Slump had spread like the plague. It was not only the labouring class that was affected; black-coated workers with years of experience and good references found themselves adrift through no fault of their own, faced with unemployment at a time when jobs were as rare as sovereigns, and when the cry of Too Old At Forty was becoming Too Old At Thirty or anyhow thirty-five. Many of these men had been drawing salaries of seven or eight hundred pounds a year, and had anticipated years more of similar employment with gradual increases and perhaps a pension when they retired. On the scale of living at that time a man with appearances to keep up, rates and taxes to pay and probably children to educate, could not hope to save much. There was always the chance of illness or some sudden emergency. But no one had supposed an emergency like this. The same story came from overseas; in Singapore the unemployed plant-ers stood about in droves. Lucky ones had their fares paid home, a good many hung about on the hope of another job materialising, a few broke under the strain of idleness and despair and took to drink.

One felt most for the men, because as a rule they had families to support, but it was bad for the women, too. I thought I had better discover the position for myself, so I put on a neat black suit, a black hat, light (but not white) gloves, shoes with moderate heels, and for the first time in years went into an employment bureau. At first, I think, I was mistaken for an employer; as soon as the mistake was discovered I was hustled over to the other side of the room.

'Yes?' said a quite uninterested voice. Probably I was the fortieth woman she had had that morning.

'I am a private secretary with eight years' experience,' I explained. 'I have also done a certain amount of journalism. Unfortunately, I am at the moment out of a post. I called to see whether you might have something suitable.'

She did not even go through the pretence of turning up a book; more ominous still, she did not even offer me a form. Such a thing had never happened to me before.

'Things are very bad just now,' she said.

'I know that,' I told her.

'The people who used to employ private secretaries are dispensing with their services and sending to us for a daily secretary once or twice in the week,' she went on. 'We have a long list of secretaries who work for us on a commission basis.'

She said it quite finally, as if to discourage me from attempting to add my name to that list. She needn't have worried; I knew what that meant. The employee got roughly a third of the fee paid; she might get a day's work this week and nothing else for a fortnight. It was a more precarious life than a casual docker's because she could not even 'sign on' and draw unemployment pay.

'Do you have no inquiries, then?' I asked.

She bridled. 'Certainly we do. But we find that prospective employers prefer girls under twenty-five. We have very few inquiries for older women.'

'So that if you have the misfortune to be thirty, or, worse still, thirty-five, you haven't a chance?'

'It's quite unusual,' she told me. 'What was your post?'

'I was secretary to an author.'

'And why did you leave?'

Why had I left? If I said because the author could no longer afford to pay my salary, it sounded bad for him. I said, 'He has gone abroad.'

'Had you been with him long?'

'Nearly six years.'

She laid down her pencil. 'Our clients prefer to mould their employees themselves. Six years with one person means you've assimilated certain ways of doing things, little tricks, whether you know it or not. That's why they prefer quite young girls. They're more adaptable.'

'What happens to them when they get to be over thirty?' I wanted to know.

'Well, some of them marry and the rest try to keep their positions, naturally.'

'But if they don't, you can't do anything for them?'

'Just at present we have very few vacancies.'

And this was one of the largest and best-advertised employment bureaux in London!

'What was the name of your employer?'

I hesitated a second and she looked at me sharply.

'Mr Gilbert – Anthony Gilbert. He writes detective stories.' He might have written advertisements for B.O. for all she had ever heard of him.

'And you were, you say, secretary to him?'

'I was everything to him,' I declared, more passionately than I had intended.

She looked at me, surprised and shocked. I was so much surprised myself that unfortunately I grinned. She stood up.

'I'm afraid we've nothing at the moment, Miss—er —er...' She had written my name and address on a corner of her blotting-pad but she did not trouble to consult the record.

'You'll let me know if anything turns up,' I pleaded, taking my gloves.

As I let myself out of the office I saw her pick up the pencil and cross out the name she had written.

That was all right for me; I didn't need a job, but London alone seethed with people who did. Since I had been at Stepney I had realised that, inadequate as the allowances often seemed, at least the labourer could pay his rent out of unemployment benefit or relief. Rent is the Old Man of the Sea to all poor families, whether they wear black coats and stiff collars or neckerchiefs. Unpaid rent is like a nightmare; and when your house is leased, not let by the week, what do you do if you are suddenly flung on the labour market with no prospect of employment?

'You see stars at first,' said one unemployed man to

me, 'and then you see sense. You realise there are only a certain number of jobs left, and in every job, like a rabbit in a hole, some other chap is crouched. What you've got to do is watch till he's off his guard and then bounce him out of his hole. The devil of it is everybody's got the wind up. Everybody's on guard now.'

Perhaps the arrival of a public-schoolboy at the office, utterly down and out, guided my thoughts. Anyhow I brooded and brooded. Who does look after the middle-class, when they are not professionals (as musicians and actors are), not old, not sick, just men in the late thirties with responsibilities they can't escape, hunting for jobs that don't exist? One man of thirty-one whom I met, who had lost his position through the rubber slump, told me that his wife had gone back to her people, he had had to take his boy from school, and he himself had been lucky enough to hear of a job starting the following month.

'A living wage?'

'Three pounds a week. Well, I can keep myself anyhow. But it isn't only that. It's the demoralising sense of not being employed …'

I knew what he meant. I had been unemployed myself. When nobody wants what you have to offer you begin to doubt your own value as a human being.

I decided to make an experiment. I would, for once, write a book round a theme, instead of round a character. My theme should be this unemployment business. My chief character should be a man of thirty-seven who, through no fault of his own, found himself on the labour market. I was working on a detective novel that had to be finished by a certain date, but as I wanted to start this other book at once I used to get up at five o'clock and work till seven on the 'sociological' book and spend the rest of the day on crime. This, however, did not go on for very long. I could not accustom myself to this new method. My plot was mapped out, but my man was a stranger. I abandoned the manuscript, devoted myself to a crime story, and went for a holiday to Yorkshire.

That autumn I had a sudden inspiration. I thought I would write a novel about a man who had committed a murder, write it from the point of view of the criminal. Most murder stories were written from the viewpoint of the police; few people seemed to realise that murderers were people like ourselves. They bought boxes of chocolates for their wives for the weekend and took their little boys to sail boats on the Round Pond on Sunday. They weren't murderers to the exclusion of everything else. My central character committed his murder by accident, and couldn't feel himself a murderer on that account. The interrelation of certain circumstances made his crime possible; if he hadn't been out of work through no fault of his own the tragedy would never have happened. At this stage I stopped dead; I realised that here I was, writing the story of the man who was the victim of the Slump. In my original version I had never thought of such an outcome; now, without my knowing it, I had discovered his private history.

I don't know how it is that some characters make so strong an impression on one's mind. Charles, the coward of the title, was everything I most dislike in men, yet he is the only character of mine with whom I have ever felt completely identified. Most of my characters seem absolutely aloof from myself, but before I had written the second chapter I would have died for Charles's peace of mind. When I was half-way through the book I turned back to the beginning and read it through. No one, I told myself reasonably, will read this book. It is extremely improbable that it will ever be published. You are a writer with a living to earn; you have not the time to spend on luxuries like this. Then I picked up the morning paper. There was a headline across the middle page: 'More Fatal Accidents on the Roads'. It appeared that the figure was rising. The thought entered my mind, 'Perhaps next week it will be you.' It seemed terrible to die without having finished the one book I desired most urgently to write. Why should I not, for once, please myself? I stubbornly settled down and completed *The Coward*. Then I put all thought of it out of my mind and began yet another story of crime and detection.

My publisher wrote in such glowing terms of *The Coward* that I put the letter under my pillow, and re-read it the next morning to make sure I had read it aright. When it was published in the summer of 1934 it received the kind of notices that all authors dream about in those dark hours when sleep seems out of the question and every lorry on earth thunders past your window. Gerald

Gould and Ralph Straus set the ball rolling on the Sunday preceding publication; other critics backed their judgement. Even James Agate devoted a whole article in the *Daily Express* to it. 'This is a remarkable novel,' he wrote in capitals right across the page, and then, in smaller type: 'One of the most remarkable things about it is that I cannot make up my mind just how good it is.' Strangers wrote to praise it, people one had never met before sat in adjacent seats at P.E.N. Club dinners and said: 'Have you read a remarkable book called *The Coward*?'

I was dazed; it seemed a refutation of all one had learned in childhood, that it was fatal to rely on pleasing oneself. Magazines and newspapers gave me contracts for serials; I sold short stories. The only thing that did not sell was the book itself; its sales remained obstinately under the two thousand mark. I was one of those unhappy authors who can please everyone except the public.

Chapter Fifteen

As soon as this book was published I was able, at last, to shake the hated dust of Ealing off my feet, I hope for ever. Back I came like a homing pigeon to London, and was lucky enough to find more or less suitable accommodation in Edwardes Square. Living in Edwardes Square is more like living in the country, with all the amenities of town, than you would believe possible. The High Street from Hammersmith Broadway to Kensington Church borders it on the north and here the traffic thunders from early morning till after midnight; on the east is Earl's Court Road, one of those roads that are used for the heavy lorries that may not travel by day. Those unwise or unfortunate enough to live in houses there tell me that the whole building shakes for the greater part of the night; yet, with all this flurry of existence around it, Edwardes Square is remote, withdrawn, as a bee in its cell. North of the garden square itself is a lover's lane, as leafy in spring as you could desire; over the back wall of Earl's Terrace laburnums droop, lilacs thrust their white and purple cones, may-trees blossom. On the south they are disfiguring the Square with flats; but behind the flats is Pear Tree Cottage, standing in its own garden, and looking as though it were isolated in a Kent orchard.

At No. 31 was born J. L. Hardy, whose book *Everything is Thunder* is one of the greatest of war novels; May Edginton used to have a house on the other side. Everybody who lives there talks about the Square as though there were no other in London, and indeed for them no others really exist. You talk to your neighbour over your garden wall, for every house there has a garden back and front; you chat over the front gates, you exchange cuttings for your little front garden. Everybody vies with everybody else to keep those gardens gay; no two gardens are ever alike. There you may find the first almond tree; there, last year, the lilac came out on the last day of March. You can even breakfast in your garden, wearing slacks and a sweater; my next-door neighbours dined in theirs in evening dress and by candlelight. Everybody has a dog, a dog of such marked individuality that it is recognised wherever it is seen.

I lived in the Square for five years, and in the first month life seemed to acquire new elements. It sparkled and promised; more, it fulfilled its promises. You could rub shoulders with it instead of getting your teeth into it. Even the Aberdeen, who had become a sober creature during his six years of suburban life, felt the change, so much so that one fine morning, when the spring was in his blood, he departed for two days and a half, and was eventually run to earth in the Lost Dogs' Home at Battersea. During those two days Square-dwellers to whom I had never spoken would come to the door and inquire about him, and when he was brought triumphantly home in the pouring rain (and a taxi-cab) one of them said serenely: 'You could tell he was one of "our" dogs; no one else would have had the sense to go to the Dogs' Home when he found he had lost his way.'

During that first autumn another unexpected thing happened to me. I became an amateur actor. There was an amateur group at the Hiawatha and I joined it under a misapprehension, thinking it was something else. When I found out my mistake saying, 'I know nothing whatsoever about acting,' I was told, cheerfully, 'You'll soon learn,' as though it was like the Greek alphabet that, intensely puzzling at first, presently becomes as obvious as the English one. At St Bride's we had had no acting opportunities such as you get at some schools. Now and again the elder pupils staged a scene from Dickens for the Annual Servants' Party and we were allowed to sit in the gallery in the gymnasium and watch, but the only step I had ever taken in this direction had been one term of 'elocution lessons', whereat I lost all caste in the eyes of the teacher by insisting on reciting a long horrific melodrama called 'The False Light of Rosilly'. I ought to have known, at the mature age of fifteen, that the proper choice was Arnold's 'A wanderer is man from his birth' or something out of Shakespeare.

My first part with the Hiawatha Amateurs was a non-speaking one. I was given a small instrument called a triangle and a little metal stick, and my task was to strike the triangle in unison with all the other members of the cast who carried similar instruments. I watched them with the most immense care, trying to judge the exact moment when all the strokes should ring out in unison, but sometimes I didn't quite make it. Some of the others didn't make it either, but after some weeks of rehearsing I put on black sateen trousers and a rose-and-gold ruff and sat on a platform, and banged for all I was worth. This was presumably, something, because presently we were asked to do it again at the New Year Party, and there was a solo 'Miss Otis Regrets' which brought down the house.

Immediately after that, it having got about that I sometimes 'wrote things', I was asked to write a charade for the Group. I prepared a very classy affair – a trial scene – in which a Hiawathan murdered a fellow-member with a carpet sharp in the Silence Room of the Club. The originality of this consisted in the member admitting liability but pleading justification. The parts were distributed one Sunday evening about twenty minutes before the performance, and I was given the part of the murderer. I had been so anxious to write in something for all the other characters that I had forgotten to give myself anything to say, and the trial must have been a unique one in criminal history, since all the accused did was to grin broadly and gibber whenever

addressed by either counsel or by the Judge. In the end
the murderer was acquitted on the ground that anyone
who has proved himself a benefactor by producing read-
able detective stories must be allowed a certain amount
of licence. In fact, the Judge congratulated him (her) on
her enterprise in putting a theory into practice before
foisting it on the public. Throughout the trial, our One
Professional Member sat in grim state in the front row,
wearing full evening dress and a red satin coat (the rest
of us had come on from Sunday supper in suburban
silkies), looking so appallingly professional that I should
have been tongue-tied in any case.

I hadn't realised, until I became an amateur myself,
the incalculable scorn with which WE were regarded by
the pros. Other professions do not have these distinc-
tions; you are a professional writer as soon as you have a
book published, even if it only sells a couple of hundred
copies. There are no amateur writers, except the Great
Unpublished, who do not count as writers at all. In our
world there are only the Successful and the Unsuccessful,
which is quite different. If you ask an amateur the main
difference between himself and a professional he will
say at once that the professional does it for a living and
is paid for it (when he is lucky enough to have a part),
while the amateur does it for fun and foots his own
expenses. This sordid money question appears to make all
the difference. Amateurs may not have many graces, but
on the other hand they had no airs. If one of our amateurs went badly astray on words and was pulled up by

a (professional) producer she always laughed merrily, to show that she saw the funny side of it; professionals never do that. Amateurs are like the Lord, in that they have no respect of persons; they don't regard a producer, even when she (I find it comes more naturally to write she) is a professional, as an Act of God. To them a producer is a person who clearly likes producing or she would not be doing it. (This, of course, is where the producer gives her services.)

Amateurs also are broad-minded. In a professional performance no one touches the stage except the stage manager, with the producer as head critic, but at an amateur rehearsal whoever arrives first will set it. As soon as the professional arrives she always twitches a chair into a different position and changes the set of a flower-vase, but that is only a professional way of emphasising her superiority. Amateurs are very open-minded folk. They are always quite ready to hear the professional's point of view about this or that movement or accent, but they like, at the same time, to give the professional the benefit of their advice, because you never know, you know, and there is a feeling that a woman who has been married and brought up children and (probably) holds a quite important position socially must have experience that will be valuable, even if she has never set foot on a professional stage. But they will always allow the professional the last word. They will explain that the turn that professionals consider *de règle* (it is either outward or inward, but I have forgotten by now which) is really not suited to them, because it is not natural. They do not wish to produce an artificial effect on the Night. They take an enormous interest in the proceedings. In professional shows only the Prompter prompts, but in amateur ones the whole cast joins in. They are very attentive to anything the producer may say about parts other than their own, and will remind her that at the last rehearsal she told Joyce or Amy or Grace to do such-and-such. They also add that if only Joyce or Amy or Grace could have done something else it would make their next move a whole lot easier; but they always give way if the professional insists. If they do not learn their words until the rehearsal before the Dress Rehearsal, it is because experience has taught them that as a rule somebody drops out at the eleventh hour, and the parts have to be shifted round. They are not proud; they never mind admitting they can't make themselves up, and are always ready to allow someone else to do this for them. In spite of what is sometimes said about them, they do turn up to as many rehearsals as they can, but after all, it is Only Fun and they can't be expected to eschew all the other fun on earth because of a mere play. Anyway, there are always plenty of other people only too glad to read their part.

Even if a show is coldly received, and they realise that this is the fault of bad production, they will never speak of this until after the show, and then only in whispers and to their best friends. And as soon as another show is mooted they are always prepared to let bygones be

bygones and accept another part. It is difficult to understand why professionals don't like amateurs more than
they do. It can't always be jealousy, as someone once
suggested to me. You would have expected them (the
professionals, I mean) to admire the way amateurs try to
discover the individuality of a character and to express it
in a way natural to themselves; this was not always well
looked upon even on the professional stage, but nowadays
the pendulum has swung a long way, and the natural
school of acting has come into its own.

Some of the Group members themselves wrote plays
for their colleagues to act. In spite of the success that
attended my charade this honour was never offered to
me. Though I would like to put it on record that later
that evening – the evening of the charade, I mean – I was
approached by a prominent member of the Authors – the
one who spoke to me about fresh blood on my first visit
– with a suggestion that we should collaborate in a play.

'You can provide the plot,' she said, 'and I will do
the characters and the dialogue, as those are my strong
points.'

'But I'm so bad at plots,' I protested, 'whereas I really
am quite good at dialogue and characterisation. All the
leading literary critics have been saying so for some years.
And anyhow,' honesty constrained me to add, 'I don't
think it would work, because if ever we had an argument
I should know I was right.'

So nothing came of that project, and in fact it was
some time before I settled down to write my first serious

three-act play. The one sent to Gerald du Maurier from the Ealing house had been a farce, and a farce of a farce at that, if you get me.

A lot of the best fun I had at the Hiawatha was with the Amateurs. After a time I was made Group Secretary, and then I saw them all from the inside. I used to sit at the Chairman's right and take minutes. I hadn't taken minutes since the days of the Central Council, and I found the Amateurs, on the whole, considerably more captious than Sir Edward Ward had been. However, I went on taking them for two years, and learning about Amateurs all the time. Take my word for it, they are like no other people on earth.

It was the summer of 1935 and of course, as the papers say, nobody was in town. In Mayfair painted shutters were closed across the windows of the houses and blinds drawn; the big silkily purring limousines, each the length of two houses, had disappeared, and with them their occupants. Even one's own friends disappeared until September. London in August is Impossible, one heard. Only now are people beginning to have sufficient courage to admit that most other places are even more so. I spent nearly all that August in London, a thing I had not done for years. Nobody in town, indeed! The town was packed. The only difference was that it was packed with a different crowd, and oh, how much more racy, more original, more unusual was this crowd! In the parks the grass was thick with men in open-necked or collarless shirts and shabby trousers, who lay about on the burnt grass letting the sun soak into them. It was a heat-wave August that year. There were queues at the tea-houses and the Kensington Lido was as full as its counterpart on the southern French coast. The children appeared, pouring out of the walls like the bugs out of the condemned houses; every chair in the Gardens was taken, and tea-trays covered the grass. Whole families spent hours with picnic-baskets or paper-parcels of food; municipal swimming baths were full to overflowing.

Those who escape from London during this month do themselves a grave disservice, for they miss entirely a phase of the city that she presents during no other month of the year. August London is cosmopolitan London; you may hear a dozen strange tongues in omnibuses and tubes – although the foreigner is a courteous person who does his best to learn a little of your language before his arrival. He helps himself out with signs and street maps, and is so pleasant and so eager to make himself understood that even the chilliest Englishman is drawn into the vortex of his attraction. In buses you would hear men who never, as a rule, spoke to those to whom they had not been introduced, directing foreigners to the British Museum, the Albert Memorial, the National Gallery. And how those foreigners brightened the town with their vivid yellow ties and cheerful blue and green coats. They had a vitality, a fund of energy that secretly appals the more slowly moving English. Go down to Victoria Station and watch them arrive, those interested vivacious men and women, who have come to discover London for themselves. Their very accents provide the jaded Londoner with a holiday; it's no wonder the policemen are nice to them. It would be difficult to be anything else. Going through the Park in the morning, walking the dog in the cool of the day, with the dew just rising from the grass, you would be stopped by little groups asking to be directed to the Peter Pan memorial; everybody wants to see that.

One afternoon the thought came to me, 'What does London look like to a stranger? Does it seem vast? beautiful? mysterious? strange?' Men in their own city are like much-married people; they never actually see their own buildings, as husbands often do not for months on end really see their wives. Suppose one had just arrived from – say – Yugoslavia – what would strike you first? It was an enchanting game. That multitude of foreign accents helped to create the illusion. All that August I also discovered London. I also discovered that I, who claimed to love the city, even its most squalid parts, knew far less about it than the tourists. I went to all the usual sights, to the pictures, to the theatre, standing in the pit queue. I found, for the first time, the little man who wears a shabby checked cap like a crooked halo, puffs out his cheeks like the sun, and plays two pipes simultaneously. He plays outside the public-house in Duke's Alley. To the people behind me he was a familiar; I felt ashamed, for even without any profound knowledge of voices, I knew this was probably their first London visit.

You get a lot of fun out of pit queues. There was the night when the woman behind me offered sixpence to a street performer, saying, in a cultured but markedly not London accent, 'Can you give me fourpence change?' There was the woman who described to her companion her chance meeting with the husband she had not seen for five years, and his suggestion that they should spend the night together for old times' sake.

'And when I told him I wasn't having any, he slapped my face, just like old times, too,' she said.

It was an eye-opener, listening to some of those queue entertainers. Many of them had had professional careers once, but bad luck or bad judgement or just the over-crowding famous to that profession had driven them to this means of getting their bread. There was a boy I heard on two successive nights reciting Hamlet's great speech, 'What a piece of work is man!' in a voice like a gong of gold, to lift an expression once used by James Agate of Martin Harvey; and at the bookstalls in St Martin's Lane there came, on those hot sunny afternoons, a collection of old men, like haggard ravens, to finger and whisper and read, men with scholars' faces gone utterly to ruin. Working, as I do, every day from nine-thirty to one, resolutely refusing to make any engagement before lunch, I was amazed at the faces all around you when you went into a Lyons' teashop for a cup of black coffee with cream at 11 a.m. They were human histories, some of those faces, telling a plain tale of some mistake in early life that caused them gradually to drop out of their own level. There was something secret and shut-up about those faces; I thought, I must be mad to sit at home as much as I do. The novelist can find twenty stories in this one room.

Naturally, at the end of ten days, my fingers itched for my typewriter. I was engaged on no particular work at the moment. As usual, I had just completed and despatched a book and was resolved to start nothing fresh until after my own holiday. At the end of the month I was going to be a tourist, not in London but in Czechoslovakia, Germany, Poland. But there were still three weeks to wait. I uncovered the machine. My story was a light and flippant affair, a totally new departure for me; into it went, like ingredients into a pot, every amusing incident, every casual encounter of the past two weeks. I had a romantic interest, an exquisite heroine, an exotic hero. I finished the book just before I packed a bag and fled to Victoria Station for my first comprehensive tour of the Continent.

It is popular among highbrows to deride those who travel on tours. Of course, they say, shrugging beautifully clad shoulders, if you aren't at home in the languages of other nations, if you're not particular as to your company, and don't mind other people making your arrangements, above all if you are able, practically speaking, to lose your way in your own house, then by all means go to Cook's or Lunn's or Hickie's or Dean and Dawson and let them take you abroad, for all the world like a member of a schoolgirl party being taken to see Shakespeare at the

Open-Air Theatre. All the above applied to me; I was enchanted at the idea of having nothing to do but write a cheque and pack a suitcase and turn up at a scheduled time. If, like Abou Ben Adhem, you love your fellow-men, you will have the time of your life on a tour.

There were the two middle-aged ladies who, having been compelled, on account of invalid parents, to live utterly uneventful lives until the middle forties, had resolved thereafter to make the most of every consequent moment, and who had, they told me, made fifty-one journeys overseas, at the rate of four a year. There was not a touring company in the country whose individualities they did not know. They warned me against the one that roused its members at 4 a.m., for a day's travel; praised the one that allowed night travelling, four to the carriage so that you had a couch for the night; they said this one was 'very mixed', the other so religious that all the members subscribed to the belief that Where There's Drink There's Danger. They told me two stories, that, they said, were first-hand. The first was about their own vicar who had been preaching on the parable of the ten virgins. Having enumerated every conceivable point on either side, he wound up: 'And now, my brethren, what are we going to do? Watch with the wise or sleep with the foolish?'

The other concerned a woman very prominent for missionary endeavours at a certain munition factory during the Great War. She held meetings every Monday night to which a large proportion of the employees were coerced to go.

'Think of the uncertainty of life,' she besought them. 'Tonight I shall sleep in my husband's bosom, but tomorrow I may be in Abraham's.'

From the back of the room came a voice. 'Got any date for Wednesday night, lady?'

There was the Irish Roman Catholic priest, who was travelling with his housekeeper, and made so much pother on the occasion in Berlin when they were not allotted adjacent rooms: so much, indeed, that Colonel P. observed with disgust, 'If the fellow doesn't like being seen ambling down the corridor in his pyjamas, can't he buy himself a dressing-gown?'

There was the lady whose suitcase was lost on the first night and who could not change her undervest throughout the tour. (It never seemed to occur to her to buy fresh garments.) There was the other who insisted on travelling so light that when she washed her underclothes or had her shoes resoled she had to spend a day in bed until they were again available; there was the Brighton Queen, a little dark fiery woman with wild hair, who complained that she had been followed all round Prague by a man, and wanted the tour to see the Consul about it. There was the young man from Cambridge, with whom I saw the night clubs of Berlin; there was the man who looked like a Victorian masher, with his whitey-yellow moustache sprucely waxed, his hair curled low over one eye and his perpetual flower in his buttonhole. He was the most knowledgeable man I have ever met, he had left a council school at the age of twelve, he was an authority on fast cutters, and he kept an antique shop just outside Cambridge. We exchanged confidences over glasses of mixed vodka and cherry brandy (costing approximately fivepence – he had two and I had three) while we were waiting for the Polish authorities to stamp our visas at the border; there was the doctor from St Mary's, Whitechapel, a district I knew well; there was the Squire and his wife, whose hobby was the breeding of Alderneys in (I think) the Isle of Wight. There was the couple from Birmingham who called everybody George; there was the one young girl over whose company everybody – every man, I mean – fought. There was the Colonel who read Hugh Walpole's *The Fortress* through miles of scenery without ever lifting his eye from the page; there were the two business gents who pushed everyone else out of the way whenever an excursion was planned, in order to get the front seats in the car.

On that trip it was simply impossible to be bored even if your novel surroundings palled. I don't know what I should have done if I had been 'on my own' when I lost my handbag in Prague and had to travel without money, tickets, passport, keys, or make-up. My companion had made me a little bag for the money and had told me to pin it inside my corsets, and when I did not take her advice I naturally received no sympathy from that quarter. But most of the husbands brought me the keys of their wives' dressing-cases in case they would fit mine – one of them did, so at least I had a shirt to sleep in – two or three said, 'Well – er – you aren't letting this worry you, are you? I mean, it'll be all right. We'll see to that,' or else simply, 'You've lots of friends on this train, and when you get back to London you've your family. We'll look after you till then,' and look after me they did until the bag turned up two or three days later, having been meticulously examined and priced by the authorities at Prague, who had extracted the amount of money they considered represented ten per cent of its value.

'I knew it would turn up,' was all I said, for had I not bought two mascots in Nuremburg, where we spent the night before Hitler's annual review, and where we had been astounded and even awed by the decorations put up in his honour – flags, banners, wreaths, photographs, copies of his books in all the shop windows, lights wherever the ingenuity of man could suggest a light being attached. These mascots were two minute pink pigs, christened after the patron saints of the two countries through which we should pass – Wenceslas and Stanislaus. When I got back to London I gave Wenceslas to Joan and Stanislaus to my father. I don't know what happened to Wenceslas, but Stanislaus still remains with us, our mascot to this day.

Oh, it was a grand trip. I was never more sorry when a holiday came to an end. London had returned to normal by this time, and in comparison with August's, London seemed quite intolerably dull.

Chapter Sixteen

I had sent the 'holiday' novel, under a title so good that I dare not repeat it here, to my agents, and they now reported that the first publishers to whom they submitted it had accepted it on very favourable terms. It came out, under a substitute title that was nothing like so arresting (I think they thought mine risky) some months later. For some reason I had anticipated that this book would sweep London. Actually it was hardly noticed by anyone, and did not sell more than three or four hundred copies. I could not help feeling that a book I had had such pleasure in writing must entertain thousands of people. I had not been so indignant about anything since my first novel collapsed before it reached its seventh hundred. However, I was now told that it had Film Possibilities. Gainsborough Pictures were interested. I might expect to hear Good News any day. The next thing I actually did hear was of the spectacular collapse of the film industry; and after that the information that an American company was interested and the book had gone out to Hollywood.

There apparently it stayed for years, for nothing else happened until one day I got a letter signed Margaret Bannerman, saying, I believe in your book. It would make a wonderful film. Come and talk to me about it.

I went and I talked, and my hopes rose again. It was like watching the stock market. One day it soared, next week something else had happened, and the bottom had dropped out. That went on for some time, until Margaret Bannerman herself went back to America. Then I resolutely put all thought of it out of my mind, and turned my attention to other things.

I was planning a long detailed novel to be founded on the Jabez Balfour case. I knew of no book that had been published on this subject, not even a history of the case itself. I rang up the publishers of *Famous Trials*, but they had done nothing; they suggested my ringing up Victor Gollancz, who had published various famous cases in omnibus form. Victor Gollancz suggested Geoffrey Bles; Geoffrey Bles suggested Simpkin Marshall; Simpkin Marshall suggested Victor Gollancz or, alternatively, Hodge's *Famous Trials*. Eventually I went to the offices of *The Times*. The trial had taken place about 1893, but Balfour's associate had been tried some years earlier. I was told that I could, for a price, inspect these records, but, if I wanted to make notes, I must go to the London Library. I had all the appropriate volumes brought down, and spent hours reading the case. It was fascinating from a novelist's point of view, and I memorised what seemed to me the salient facts. I had been at this for about an hour, sitting in a roaring draught, when I realised I was beginning one of my famous colds. I put the thought away. Thought is the root of all evil, I had been told. I concentrated on the amazing Mr Balfour. By the time I had finished the case, I was dizzy and light-headed. I left *The Times* office and went into a cafe. I hoped, by drinking quantities of hot black coffee to stave off the cold. However, it was no good; for five days I was laid low with a burning throat, blazing head, aching eyeballs. I tossed feverishly, wondering how to start the book. My first chapter is always my Rubicon. Once I am over that I can proceed, but I will write a first chapter twenty times, eighteen of them beginning the story at a different stage.

The Gambler was a long book and took a very long time to write. About now violent discussions would ensue between Miss Malleson and Mr Gilbert, who felt that his less erudite work was being ruthlessly thrust against the wall.

'Who pays the rent and settles the grocer's bill?' Mr Gilbert demanded truculently.

'Well, you do, of course, but ...'

'Who had the kitchen repainted and bought the dog's licence?'

'I know you do more than I do about the house ...'

'More? You don't do a thing, except buy clothes you can't afford and waste money in that ridiculous club of yours.'

'You've been writing longer than I have ...'

'And now you expect to have nine full months to

write a novel that probably won't net a hundred pounds, and I have to produce two in that time. If I want the typewriter while you're working I have to wait till midnight and get any scrappy attention that's going then.'

'But my sort of book takes longer to write. Ask any one.'

'If they're not economically justified...'

Lucy (almost in tears), 'There's more to life than economic justification.'

'Tell that to the tax collector.'

Lucy (sulkily), 'If I earn as little as you say, I can't be liable for income tax.'

'Of course you're not. They lump your ridiculous earnings in with mine, and make me pay on the two. It's as bad as being your husband.'

The only amicable way out of the squabble was to hand over the typewriter to Mr Gilbert for two consecutive detective novels, and then Lucy Malleson could have it until her book was done. This spacing of novels is a difficult affair. You assume that if you deliver a book by a certain date it will be published (and your advance paid) by another fixed date; but it's an uncertain world. Your story may be postponed by a couple of months for some unforeseeable reason; occasionally it is put off until the beginning of the new season. The effect on your affairs is the same as though a dividend were suddenly postponed, assuming you to be the kind of person whose dividends are always mortgaged by the time they arrive. Two months' delay means you have to send your charwoman to cash your cheques, for fear of that suave bank manager's voice (how well we all know it!) saying, 'Could you spare me a few minutes, Miss N. or M.?' And you cross the street as you approach your milliner's, in case Madame should chance to be at the door and murmur, 'I have the very thing for you. You must just come in and try it on,' a ladylike way of saying she would like something on account.

As soon as I had finished *The Gambler* I went abroad again, to Dubrovnik this time, travelling third-class all across Europe, staying a couple of days at Venice, a couple of days at Verona (where I got food poisoning), and so on to the town that was Ragusa on our maps at school, arriving at dusk in the big harbour, driving under ancient archways to the hotel up the hill that looked over the Aegean Sea. I discovered for the first time what the colour of plumbago was, and got badly burned, and lay about for days in a long chair writing bastard rhymes to send home. There was an alphabet, entitled *Voyage en Style*, whose best couplet was:

> *M's Macaroni, poor Anthony's Waterloo,*
> *They snatch it away before he's a quarter through.*

Then I came back to find about forty letters waiting for me, among them one from the publisher accepting *The Gambler.* So next morning Mr Gilbert took command and began *The Man Who Wasn't There.*

★

Edna Ferber in her fascinating autobiography says that the life of the successful writer differs little in fact from the life of the man who is hanging on by his eyelids. Success or failure, he is to be found at his typewriter every morning, and most of yesterday's work is forgotten, for all one's attention is for today and all one's hope for tomorrow. And it's true that, while you work, you forget the dozens of disappointments behind you and the morass of anxiety in which you are at this moment stumbling, and concentrate on the job in hand for all the world as though you earned your five thousand a year with the bestsellers.

'Don't ask me whether I am writing a book,' Berta Ruck once implored me. 'I am always writing a book.'

Indeed, most of us are not alive when we do not write, and if you told us that we were going to be compelled for any reason to abandon our work, on that day we should begin to die. Indeed, when I come to die, if there is any one left who feels inclined to put up a little memorial, I would rather have a typewriter put on my tomb than all the broken pillars, crushed buds and hands-pointing-heavenward that have ever disfigured every cemetery in the world. And it need only be quite a small typewriter, because, though I don't expect to be remembered as anything but an author, I don't even expect to be remembered very much as that.

Well, having despatched the novel to the Crime Club, it seemed to me that here was an ideal occasion, between light and light as it were, to produce a play. No one can

altogether explain why play-writing, even when you're
not successful, should be so fascinating, but it is a fact that
almost every author who gets a play produced (novelist-
author, I mean) tends to give more and more attention to
the stage and less and less to the work of writing novels.
Anyhow, the charm exists. I used to read my acts over
and over to the dog, one eye on the clock, half my attention given to possible byplay, already seeing myself in a
long silver tissue gown, bowing acknowledgements on
my first night. The history of the play was devastatingly
commonplace. It went, via an agent, to a good many
managers, who returned it with monotonous unanimity.
At last it came back to me.

I flung it into a drawer, feeling for it neither affection
nor tenderness. I do not like failures; I know they are
sometimes inevitable, but I consider they should keep out
of the limelight. I hate my own failures as I would hate
a wart or anything else disfiguring. As for the failures
that are deliberately 'gallant', these make me feel like
Ortheris in the pass. (And what turns my stummick ain't
no blinkin' vi'lets neither.) I just didn't burn the play, I
don't know why. Probably I hadn't time at the moment.
And there it stayed for months and months and months.
Then, turning out some papers, I found it again. The
previous day I had had tea with a friend who was also a
member of the Great Unproduced.

'It has just come back again,' she told me. 'I sent it to
John Gielgud, and he returned it with such a nice letter.'

I saw no reason why I, also, should not have a nice

letter from Mr Gielgud. So I hooked it out of its drawer, did it up in a bit of brown paper, with four three-halfpenny stamps enclosed, and sent it to the Queen's Theatre.

It is absurd to say, as disgruntled people sometimes do, that actor-managers do not read plays by unknown writers. Within three weeks of the date of posting I came back in the early hours of the morning to find a letter on my eiderdown. It was from Mr Gielgud, and it was all about my play. He liked the play; he thought it was original; he thought the dialogue vivid and unusual; he would like to produce it (not at all the same thing as back it, by the way) for a Sunday Society; he had the exact young actor in mind to play the chief part; he didn't see why it shouldn't be as successful as (a play that had been running for nearly two years). If I liked this idea, what about coming to see him one evening before the show?

I had never been to a star's dressing-room, though I had been behind the scenes at the Playhouse when a friend of mine, Margery Bryce, was playing in *White-oaks*. I shook with accumulated nervousness and excitement. Now I was not only bowing acknowledgements in a silver tissue gown, I was deciding with knitted brows on the best investments for my earnings. Mr Gielgud was making up for his part in *The Three Sisters*; he went on making up while he talked. I saw that young man's face change under my eyes. I was fascinated, so fascinated that I only listened to what he was saying with a part of my mind. I was imagining how I'd dress this story up when I told it.

'When I was chatting to John Gielgud in his dressing-room the other day ...'

'As John Gielgud said to me last week ...'

Mr Gielgud was explaining that the play was under-written, but that was a fault easily remedied; he had shown it to a young actor who was keen to play the hero's part; he was going to show it to a young producer who had, he said, a pull with some of the Sunday Societies; he had thought of the perfect girl for the chief woman's part. He said he supposed I hadn't thought the play would be any use to him as a vehicle for acting, because 'I have so much personality I should blow the thing to smithereens. Your young man is extremely ordinary. You do realise that?'

That was almost the greatest triumph of the evening. For the play was written round my favourite theme – King Charles's Head it is to me – that a murderer is a man like everybody else, unassuming, unremarkable, living the usual small-town existence, utterly out of the public eye until, usually through some accident or sheer bad luck, the eyes of thousands are focused upon him. So I said demurely, yes, I quite realised that and the talk went on.

When I got back I rushed in to tell Joan the story.

'Did you,' she inquired interestedly, 'put your elbows on the table like that?'

'I expect I did,' I admitted guiltily, remembering those

sundry occasions of youth when a stern elder reached out and bumped one's elbow sharply on the hard wooden surface to teach you that little ladies never sat like that. 'I don't suppose he minded,' I added.

'It isn't that,' said Joan, 'but you do realise that both the elbows of your fur coat have come through.'

I looked; yes, it was quite right. The black velvet coat was only too clearly discernible when I bent my arm. He couldn't have helped seeing, I supposed.

I felt badly about this. I thought for a time, then went to see my pet furrier.

'What can you do with this?' I inquired.

She said gently, 'It has worked hard, hasn't it?'

'Of course I'd love a new one, but I couldn't possibly pay for it for six months.'

She went away, returning an instant later with a little soft wrap coat in dyed musquash, one of those coats that are kind to the not-so-young face, that smooth away curves that you are beginning to think may be just a little too Victorian. Oh, a peach of a coat, the sort of coat that seems to invest its wearer with the charm you have admired and envied in others for so long.

'It's perfect,' I sighed.

'It doesn't need a thing doing to it,' she agreed. 'And I could send it out this afternoon.'

'Six months,' I repeated, my hands in the slit fur pockets with their cunning brown velvet linings. I couldn't bear to take my hands out or feel that lovely weight lifted off my shoulders.

'The collar turns up, so, if you wish,' she said. She smiled like all the angels on high. 'What a fortunate thing you have an account with us, madam. Otherwise it might have been a little difficult to arrange matters.'

Six months later, almost to the day, I sent her a cheque.

Of course I know what the end of this story about the play ought to be. It ought to have been produced by a Sunday Society with the cast Mr Gielgud had suggested, been a roaring success, and still be packing houses here and on Broadway. But half life's fun is its unexpectedness. None of the Sunday Societies would back the play; some sent it back in three weeks, some in three months. One night during the following September I was spending a weekend in the country. We arrived in the remotest spot on earth at about ten-thirty; the only house near us was dark, but on a watering-can outside the garage was a pencilled note: 'Please ring up your home address as soon as you arrive.'

I stole into the dark house, feeling like a burglar. I called my number. Joan's voice said, 'John Gielgud wants your play back.' I described the exact position of the play in my workroom. It went off by registered post the next morning. But although Gielgud had offered to do the producing, nobody was unselfishly prepared to lose quite a large sum of money putting on a play that wouldn't run; and once more it came home to roost.

So I am still in the ranks of unsuccessful dramatists. Still, I protest that a play that has attracted the attention of one of our leading actor-managers is emphatically not in the same category as a play that has merely gone the rounds and returned with enough rejection slips to paper a cupboard. And I shall go on thinking so until one day Mr Gielgud or somebody else really puts on a play of mine, after which I can afford to disregard this very minor achievement. The new play, in fact, has just been done and is setting forth on its rounds, and this play may be the turning-point of my career. That's one of the cheerful things about work like ours. If, like me, you still are incorrigibly optimistic, if you know in your heart of hearts that Providence intended you for a success and your main desire in life is to assist Providence to this end, why then you will never see a book with your name on the spine without the eager thought, 'This may be it. This probably is.' And when the book sells no more copies than its predecessor, well, by that time you're always neck-deep in another one, and this one, without doubt, will bring you that elusive fame and financial security that glimmer like distant stars on the far, far horizon.

Doubtless there is much in what Robert Louis Stevenson says about it being better to travel than to arrive, but one would like to arrive just once. After all, you could always start out again next morning for somewhere else.

I came back to London in the September of 1938 in time for the crisis. I found a notice in my letter-box asking me to apply for my gas-mask at once. I went round to my local office, and was fitted; subsequently I received one a size too large, and was asked how many more I wanted. At the same time my father went to the office and got another, so we had a mask for nearly every room of the house. There was a mass meeting at the Town Hall; it was advisable to go early as it was sure to be crowded. I made a note of the time. Then, suddenly, I rebelled. I went to see my hairdresser; I bought a ravishing and unexpectedly becoming new hat. I rang up the Duchess Theatre and bought a stall for *The Corn is Green*. If war was to be declared at midnight, as everyone expected, at least I would have one good day to remember. On my way home I thought, 'Well, at least I've seen those two. I shan't forget their performance, even in the middle of a war.'

And there wasn't a war after all, not then.

This spring I had a chance to go to the south of France for a couple of weeks, if I could find the fare. I found it in a number of unconventional ways, and spent my last day in England assuring anxious inquirers on the telephone that I really was going in the morning, in spite of the unpromising conditions in Central Europe. Nobody at La Lavandou ever seemed to have heard of a war. We bathed and motored and walked, and I practised my bad French on the natives, with sometimes surprising results, and had my hair cut and curled and coloured so that I wasn't recognised at the first party I went to on my return. And Mr Gilbert began a new book and Miss Malleson looked for a new flat. And then out of the blue came Margaret Bannerman for the second time.

Miss Bannerman still believed in the film possibilities of that romantic novel. More, she had discovered someone else who saw them, too. We might get together, she and I and the script writer from Hollywood, and together make other people realise what we knew already. She asked me to lunch.

Miss Bannerman has a flat in Park Lane, on the eighth floor. Going to lunch with any one like that makes you feel like a super in a luxury film. You shoot up until the trees in the Park are far below you; the taxis are like toys. The flat has a sun lounge, framed in glass, and a television set. You stand together on the balcony.

'I always think there's something to be done with a story about taxi-cabs,' Miss Bannerman murmurs. 'Look at them – a long string. You could do something with that.'

Distance does not only lend enchantment to the view, it lends an original conception of the commonplace. No one could have thought of that from a ground floor window.

'I hope you'll like this sweet,' says Margaret Bannerman, as we have lunch. 'I saw it on television yesterday – it's by Boulestin.'

The sweet comes in. It is a huge cantaloupe melon with the lid removed; the pulp has been taken out and mixed with two peaches, a basket of strawberries and a basket of raspberries; the whole is returned to the interior of the cantaloupe, the strawberries being kept whole, and the melon is put in the icebox. When it is ice-cold it is served with sugar and cream.

All good hostesses appreciate an eager guest; quite half the interior of that melon found its way to my plate. (Gosh, Lucy, is this really you, lunching with a West End actress in her Park Lane flat? Oh, it's true that fact is stranger than fiction. Imagination had never soared to this.) Then we got together – in fact, we are still getting together and the scenario is another big Perhaps. Meanwhile, Mr Gilbert, clinging to the typewriter, is wondering desperately how on earth the man knew that body was in the cellar; when he knows that for himself, he can explain it to his readers; and Lucy is getting more and more aware of a man, no longer young, with an intense unforgettable face who began to make his existence known weeks ago and is gradually becoming clearer to the view – for that's the way most books are begun. And any day now the familiar tussle for the typewriter will begin. Ah well, it's all very stimulating while it lasts, and one hopes it may go on for ever.

One thing about writing for a living is that it leaves you very little time for those mystical self-communings that are so destructive of sound work. You know the kind of thing, because so many authors admittedly have these overwhelming qualms of self-distrust and a sense of their own futility.

'What's it all about?' they ask themselves. 'What have you got to show for so much effort, so many years of living? Just a row of books, that's all. It isn't even as though they were great books that would be remembered by posterity; why, not one of them has been a bestseller. None of them ever achieved a five-figure circulation; you've never been chosen by the Book Society or even the *Evening Standard*. Nobody ever thought of awarding you the Hawthornden, let alone the Nobel Prize. Other people at least leave a child or so behind them to mark the space they occupied in life, but you – you go out like a burst bubble. Isn't it rather silly to be so serious and so excited about it all?'

No, I don't believe it is. I think it's much sillier to be one of those people who are never enormously serious or excited about anything. And it isn't any author's job to produce bestsellers or even to win the Hawthornden. You obviously can't be responsible for your public. You can (I speak, naturally, for the writers who do take their work seriously) only write the books that are yours to write. And your circulation must take care of itself. Nine-tenths of it is luck anyway. A publisher once told me that if he knew what books would be popular and what would fail to interest the public, he would be a rich man. The important thing, as I see it, is to stick to your last, through all vicissitudes, to become, some time or other, the thing that you intended eventually to be.

I don't feel guilty that my books don't sell ten thousand copies, though I should love them to, and so would my publishers. When I was young I confidently thought they would; when they didn't I was astounded, but it never occurred to me, when my average sales were 1,250 copies, to abandon writing and do something more lucrative. Besides, one day they may.

If this were a Victorian record with a double title I should have called it: *Perhaps – the Portrait of an Author*. Perhaps is to me what Calais was to Queen Mary. Perhaps my play will be produced, perhaps something will come of the scenario, perhaps my next book will set the Thames on fire. Perhaps fame is only just round the corner. Isn't it said of Bernard Shaw that he began his really memorable work at forty? That's one reason why writing is such fun – it's so chancy. And I wouldn't exchange my one-chance-in-a-million for anybody else's security. In short, I like being a writer, which is just as well, as I clearly could not be anything else. I like the thought of all the books I don't know anything about yet, that one day I shall write. I like the realisation that tomorrow morning I shall start on a fresh book – for I mean to finish this tonight. In fact, I like my own life. For all its queer shape (and it isn't remotely what I intended it to be) at least it is obviously mine – I mean, it couldn't be just anyone's. And though I would not for an instant suggest that I'm proud of it, most certainly I'm glad of it.

> *Thank God for life!*
> *Life is not good always,*
> *Hands may be heavy-laden, hearts care-full,*
> *Unwelcome nights follow unwelcome days,*

And dreams divine end in awakenings dull,
Still, it is life, and that is cause for praise.
This ache, this restlessness, this quickening sting,
Prove me no torpid and inanimate thing,
Prove me of Him who is of life the spring.
I am alive and that is beautiful.
July 1939.